"Our age is fixated on techniques. Yet the beautifully crafted sermon that exalts the preacher over Christ is actually the ugliest sermon of all. Adapting the wisdom of the Westminster Shorter Catechism, *The Preacher's Catechism* draws us back to what really matters. But make no mistake: the result is profoundly practical. You can read it as a primer or dip in for fresh insight or inspiration. All the way, you'll find plenty to inform, challenge, and encourage your preaching."

Tim Chester, Pastor, Grace Church Boroughbridge, North Yorkshire; Faculty Member, Crosslands Training

"*The Preacher's Catechism* is a book from the heart that candidly reflects Allen's own experience of the ups and downs of the preaching ministry. He writes in an engaging and fresh style that provokes thought. Here we find that preachers are 'heavy lifters' who need the 'Monday gospel.' This book will repay slow and reflective reading by preachers. It will foster the joyful obedience of a preacher, but also expose the activity of his flesh in all its ugliness. Take a little dose at a time and ponder it. Find in it pointers to the remedy for both pride and discouragement. I pray that the Lord will use it to bring down the proud in us all, and then to lift up the humble."

Garry J. Williams, Director, The Pastor's Academy, London Seminary; author, *His Love Endures Forever* and *Silent Witnesses*

"This book is entirely different from any other. It is directed at the preacher himself rather than the art and craft of preaching, and is all the more useful for it. For too long we have focused on the method at the expense of the man. Allen's creative and content-rich volume goes a long way toward redressing the balance while marrying a familiar format with fresh insight. Every preacher of the Word of God will benefit from spending time in this volume and letting its lessons seep into his bloodstream."

Adrian Reynolds, Training Director, The Fellowship of Independent Evangelical Churches

"These warmhearted and practical devotions could also be titled *The Preacher's Comfort*. Allen gets inside the pastor's head and points him to Jesus Christ in a way that will soothe and strengthen many a weary preacher's soul."

Joel R. Beeke, President, Professor of Systematic Theology and Homiletics, Puritan Reformed Theological Seminary; Pastor, Heritage Reformed Congregation, Grand Rapids, Michigan

"We live in a Corinthian society, where preaching is regarded as foolishness by both the religious and the nonreligious. We also live in a quick-fix society, where even preaching is considered something that can easily be done. Lewis Allen's ingenious book is an antidote to both of those perspectives—insightful, realistic, biblical, clear, and contemporary. I will buy it and use it with preachers I train!"

David Robertson, Minister, St. Peter's Free Church, Dundee, Scotland; Editor, *The Record*; Associate Director, Solas Centre for Public Christianity

"Preaching is soul business, and the souls of godly preachers are under continual assault from the world, the flesh, and the Devil. In my last ten years of ministry, I have not read any resource that has so convicted and challenged my soul as has Lewis Allen's *The Preacher's Catechism*. His creative and detailed application of the theological riches of the Westminster Shorter Catechism to every area of a preacher's soul and practice will continue to feed and protect my ministry for years to come. I will return to it again and again."

Andy Davis, Senior Pastor, First Baptist Church, Durham, North Carolina

"The weakness of much contemporary preaching stems not primarily from a lack of exegetical technique or presentational skill but from the inadequate spiritual preparation and flawed motives of the preacher. Lewis Allen's new book will challenge preachers to ensure that they proclaim the Word of God with a prayerful desire to see God faithfully disclosed and glorified for who he is, out of a love for his people. Forty-three short chapters apply the core teaching of the Westminster Shorter Catechism specifically to preachers with clarity and insight. Any preacher who reads this book will be humbled, stimulated, challenged, and equipped for the glorious task of preaching, and encouraged to have a deep trust in the power of the Word and the sufficiency of God in this labor. The format is designed for preachers to read alone, perhaps as a daily meditation, but would also be ideal for use by preaching groups, ministers fraternal, or staff teams that want to improve the quality of their preaching."

John Stevens, National Director, The Fellowship of Independent Evangelical Churches

"Preachers often work hard to catechize others, but rarely think about being catechized themselves. This is an excellent resource to help us do just that, and I commend it warmly. It's just the kind of book I will use with my preaching team."

Robin Weekes, Minister, Emmanuel Church, Wimbledon

The Preacher's Catechism

The Preacher's Catechism

Lewis Allen

Foreword by
Sinclair B. Ferguson

 CROSSWAY®

WHEATON, ILLINOIS

Hardcover ISBN: 978-1-4335-5935-8
ePub ISBN: 978-1-4335-5938-9
PDF ISBN: 978-1-4335-5936-5
Mobipocket ISBN: 978-1-4335-5937-2

Library of Congress Cataloging-in-Publication Data

Names: Allen, Lewis, 1971– author.
Title: The preacher's catechism / Lewis Allen; foreword by Sinclair B. Ferguson.
Description: Wheaton: Crossway, 2018. | Includes bibliographical references and index.
Identifiers: LCCN 2017056420 (print) | LCCN 2018020805 (ebook) | ISBN 9781433559365 (pdf) | ISBN 9781433559372 (mobi) | ISBN 9781433559389 (epub) | ISBN 9781433559358 (tp)
Subjects: LCSH: Preaching—Miscellanea. | Pastoral theology—Miscellanea.
Classification: LCC BV4211.3 (ebook) | LCC BV4211.3 .A4243 2018 (print) | DDC 251—dc23
LC record available at https://lccn.loc.gov/2017056420

Crossway is a publishing ministry of Good News Publishers.

LB		28	27	26	25	24	23	22	21	20	19	18
15	14	13	12	11	10	9	8	7	6	5	4	3	2	1

To Sarah

Contents

Part 4   Preaching with Conviction

Foreword

If you are a pastor picking up *The Preacher's Catechism*, intrigued by the title, your first reaction may be: "Do preachers need to be catechized? I thought that was for children—in ye olden days!" But that reaction may soon turn to: "What a great idea! Why didn't I think of it?" For in these pages you will find not only instruction but also a kind of traveling companion along the pilgrimage of ministry—one that, like a child, will keep asking you fundamental questions but then, like a wise friend, will point you to biblical answers, and in this way encourage you to reflect on what it means to be a preacher of the gospel.

Composing a catechism is no mean accomplishment (try it; you will find it much more difficult than you imagined). Where do you begin—with God, with Scripture, with Christ, or with the human predicament? And how do you answer one question in a way that leads logically to the next? It is because the great catechisms express both biblical and theological logic so well that one of their remarkable effects is to teach catechumens how to think. This explains in part why the Christian communities that have used them have often been the seedbeds for men and women who have made remarkable contributions to a great many aspects of life.

I mention this because in our contemporary world, where we suffer from information overload, there is a tremendous need for us—yes, pastors included (and perhaps pastors especially)—to learn how to stop and think, and to be able to think things through from biblical first principles. I hope that Lewis Allen's *The Preacher's Catechism* will be an encouragement in that direction and a real help to all of us who preach. It asks the questions we should have asked ourselves—if only we had thought about it!

Lewis Allen may be less well known to readers in North American than he is in the United Kingdom. Following his studies in classics and theology at the University of Cambridge, he served for twelve years in Gunnersbury Baptist Church in West London. In 2010 he and his wife, Sarah, sensed a call to a very different sphere of ministry and became church planters in Huddersfield in Yorkshire. Over the years, he has been heavily involved in the leadership of various "gospel partnerships," as they have become known, especially in England. He therefore brings a wide and varied experience of pastoral ministry and ministers, a keen intellect, and infectious enthusiasm to these pages. Above all, he brings to them a desire to help others as he himself has been helped by others—both by personal conversation with preachers in the present day and by reading preachers from the past.

The Preacher's Catechism is not merely a book to be speed-read in one sitting—although doing so proves worthwhile. Rather, it is a book for a whole lifetime of ministry, one to which the preacher can turn again and again to be refreshed, strengthened, challenged, instructed, corrected, and encouraged to keep on going, and to seek to do better for the Lord. There are surely few more challenging words for the preacher than Paul's to Timothy, "Practice these things, immerse yourself in them, *so that all may see your progress*" (1 Tim. 4:15). *The Preacher's Catechism* should help us do precisely that.

Some years ago, I watched a BBC documentary about a distinguished microbiologist honored by the Queen for her services to medical science. She had devoted her research to studying the mutation of one particular virus. As a result of her work, the UK government had given permission for experimental medical injection procedures to be carried out on people who, because of inoperable conditions, had only a few weeks left to live. The results were remarkable—in some instances verging on the miraculous. She was also a long-standing friend and a member of the congregation I served. When I congratulated her on the documentary, I said how satisfying it must be to have devoted her career to something that had accomplished so much good. She responded in a way that spoke volumes about her priorities: "What I do isn't really all that important. But *what you do, that's really important.*"

Preaching, more important than making a life-extending contribution to medical science? My friend thought so. So should I. So should you. My hope and prayer for *The Preacher's Catechism* is that it will sustain, refresh, and, if necessary, recover that vision.

Sinclair B. Ferguson

Introduction

The Preacher's Catechism is a book for busy preachers, young and experienced, whether bursting with enthusiasm or fighting cynicism, full-time or part-time. Preaching, the declaring of God's eternal Word to time-bound but eternal creatures, is serious work, and its triumphs and disasters echo into eternity. We have the most glorious calling on earth, but it's maybe also the hardest. Preaching really matters.

Every preacher needs to improve his preaching. We should work at our exegesis of the text of Scripture and aim to teach practically and helpfully. We must learn to present Christ in all of the Scriptures in ways that encourage faith and joy in him. We need to work hard with our choice of words and illustrations in order to serve the message we are bringing people. Preachers who don't commit to keeping on learning will end up saying the same things in the same ways. Predictable sermons bless few, if any.

You can, by God's grace, learn to do all these things necessary to improve. And yet, having all of these tools will not ensure that you are a preacher after God's own heart, someone who is really serving those who listen to you. Skills have an essential place, but more essential to our calling are a heart and mind captivated by God and his gospel. Know and enjoy him, and you will really be sharing a lasting legacy through your preaching. People will see that the God you speak of is real. This book is an attempt to add to that equipping.

Three Basic Convictions

What we're doing here is based on three convictions, which we'll explore briefly before they're worked through in the chapters. The first is that preaching is a commission to a life of fruitful and joyful service in declaring the whole counsel of God. The second is that we will best fulfill our commission by becoming better acquainted with the work of preaching and our own inner lives. The third is that help for preachers is at hand in the Westminster Shorter Catechism. Put them together, and you have the Preacher's Catechism.

Conviction 1: The church needs preachers who last and thrive. We live in a short-term world. The modern workplace gives no guarantee of any job, let alone the jobs-for-life our grandparents had. We are mobile, and most people are looking for the next thing. Sticking to the task of preaching, year in, year out, and maybe in the same place, is seen as a bit quaint, an acceptable lifestyle for the old-fashioned or the risk-averse. And yet, this is the very thing we are called to. We must last, and more than last, we must thrive.

We must learn to outlive our conflicting feelings in ministry, including the urges to take ourselves elsewhere when ministry gets tedious or troublesome. We need to make it a top priority to work out how we will stay faithful to the task and to the congregation the Lord has assigned to us.

A fruitful ministry comes from the heart of a contented preacher. It's not about getting your life circumstances right (be that church, salary, peer recognition, or work-life balance). Some of the most impacting ministries have been carried out through truly wretched situations, filled with years of stress and opposition. So many preachers have stood firm and persevered with fruit owing to their deep heart contentment in the God of the gospel. Christ must be a treasure of ever-deepening worth to us.

We know this, don't we? Jesus must be everything to us. Don't we preach to others that he, not success or recognition or comfort, is what discipleship is all about? Of course we do. And yet, this truth can so easily get lost in the joys as well as the disasters of preaching. Every preacher wrestles with life's struggles, but every preacher is called to find a joy in Jesus Christ that grows as the years go on. A dry and joyless preacher is a burden, at best. A preacher whose pulpit freshness comes from a living relationship with Jesus is a great blessing to the church. Our catechism seeks to help us make sure that Jesus is the center of our lives, and then of our ministry.

Conviction 2: Preachers must understand how preaching works, and how their own souls work. Our work as preachers is devilishly difficult. Satan hates all of God's servants, maybe preachers most of all. Satan has always attacked those who bring God's Word. He began his assaults in the garden of Eden, on Adam and Eve, who were charged to listen to and bring God's word to the world, and the signs are that he has not given up. Of all his subtle attacks against us, two stand out: the temptation we have to undervalue the majesty and power of preaching, and the temptation to overlook the deep needs of our own souls.

It seems surprising that we preachers, of all people, should undervalue our calling. The evidence bears out that we do, though. We put plenty of effort into our preaching, but the rewards of radically transformed lives among our hearers are just not what we have hoped, prayed, and worked for. Sermons disappoint us, they miss their marks, and they sometimes fail to achieve much, if anything. Christians seem to change little, and unbelievers aren't converted. We pray, preach, preach again (and again), and anxiously wait for fruit. When nothing appears to happen, what preacher doesn't struggle with discouragement, and doesn't wonder if all this preaching is really worth it? The Devil loves a discouraged preacher, and his infernal crosshairs are always trained on us.

So we press on as best we can. God gloriously uses these hard seasons of ministry to strengthen us. There is another power at work, though: the power of discouragement. Under the surface, hidden even from our fretting thoughts, there are unseen currents working to erode our spiritual joy and assurance. John Bunyan once sensed that the Devil was speaking to him. Satan was very happy with his youthful zeal and wasn't at all intimidated by it. Satan's plan, Bunyan heard, was to cool him "by degrees," slowly but surely. As long as this young enthusiast ended up cold, cynical, and self-protecting, the Tempter would be happy. "Though you be burning hot at present, yet, if I can pull you from this fire, I shall have you cool before it be long."[1] Does he have a different strategy for God's servants today? No. This one works so well. If we are to be effective, we must be aware of it.

Even in our hectic age, we need to remember that almost all spiritual work—whether from heaven or hell—works slowly. We are changed over time. Preaching does work, but so often it works slowly. We need to make sure that we will still be around to be part of that work of God and to see its fruits. We must be content to press on.

Those who keep going in their preaching ministry do so only as they learn to nurture their own souls. Even the strongest of us are fragile men. It's not enough to preach grace; we need it ourselves. We need to understand our souls so that we can look after them. Our calling isn't primarily to preach to others. Like every other Christian, we preachers must preach to ourselves. If we are to do this well, we must learn to recognize the dangers that lurk, even in the work of ministering the Word. Exhaustion, elation, personal

---

1. John Bunyan, *Grace Abounding to the Chief of Sinners*, in *The Works of John Bunyan*, vol. 1, *Experimental, Doctrinal and Practical*, ed. George Offor (Edinburgh: Banner of Truth, 1991), 19.

spiritual growth, pride, and despair all feature in our work. How do we recognize them? How do we respond to them? This is what we'll be looking at.

Conviction 3: The Westminster Shorter Catechism is an outstanding resource for the heart needs of every preacher. Catechisms are almost as old as Christianity. In the early Christian centuries a catechism (from the Greek word meaning "teaching") was a body of Bible truths to be taught to children and new converts. The form developed into a series of questions and answers, often to be recited aloud and committed to memory. The Reformation saw numbers of catechisms produced, and a good number of them are still used around the world today, as they put essential gospel teaching in clear and memorable language.

A catechism is an excellent way of helping people to engage with and reflect on Christian truth. Pithily worded questions and answers lodge in the mind and sink into the heart. There they can take root, and over the years a believer can appreciate their meaning more deeply. It is interesting that in our word-crowded world, more churches are seeking out historic catechisms, or are writing their own, to enable them to enjoy and to pass on the message of the gospel.

The Westminster Shorter Catechism (yes, there is a larger one) was published in 1647. Over one hundred pastors and educators met in London for sessions of study and conversation in order to frame doctrinal statements and directives for church government that they hoped would serve the national church in Great Britain. The achievements from the eventual ten years of meetings were far-reaching: the gatherings (known collectively as the Westminster Assembly), produced a confession of faith, two catechisms, and documents on public worship and church government. These have formed the governing documents of almost every English-speaking Presbyterian church, and have been used across the world since their first publication. Arguably the most used of them today is the Shorter Catechism.

The Westminster Shorter Catechism was written to meet the needs of the whole church. For centuries it has been used to train children and adults in their gospel faith. How about us preachers? We have much to learn from the catechism, both as disciples and as disciples with a particular calling to preach the Word of God.

A Catechism for Preachers

The Preacher's Catechism is indebted to the Westminster Shorter Catechism in its question-and-answer format and its overall structure. But it's also significantly different. The 107 Westminster questions become 43. Every one of our questions and answers is reworded, in order to explore the priority of preaching and of the preacher's own needs. What we have is an entirely new catechism, though one much indebted to its noble ancestor.

The Preacher's Catechism is a catechism for preachers. I have in my sights those called to full-time Word ministry. I also want to engage the whole range of preachers, including those starting out and testing a call, ministry students, and those gifted to preach but not called to the pastorate. The focus is mainly on Sunday pulpit ministry. Preaching has its many forms, of course, and this catechism is for all of us who handle God's Word in a variety of contexts. If you pick up the Bible with the aim of bringing its message to others in some sort of public setting, this book is for you. In it we take time to explore what it looks and feels like to be a preacher of God's Word.

I've tried to preach for nearly as long as I've been a Christian. Some of the disasters of those early years are forever etched into my memory. "Keen but clueless" would describe at least my first fifty church sermons. Still, my hearers exercised the grace of forgiveness, and because no one actually forced me to stop, I didn't, and haven't. A call to the pastorate in my midtwenties began twelve and a half years' very happy pastoring in London. The Lord then surprised me, my family, and the church by issuing us a clear call to leave that happy community and cross cultures to Huddersfield, West Yorkshire, to plant what was to become

Hope Church from scratch in 2010. All the way the preaching of God's Word has been at the center of my ministry and at the heart of changed lives through that ministry.

One of the deep joys of ministry is that we get to share the task with fellow preachers. Three friends whose preaching I gladly sit under have read this book in its later stages. Sinclair Ferguson, Robin Weekes, and Garry Williams each gave their time to read my chapters and offered very astute comments. They deserve a huge debt of thanks for their wise heads and generous hearts. I'm also very grateful to Thom Notaro and the whole Crossway team, whose enthusiasm for the book and hard work have been such an encouragement to me.

My family has made a lot of sacrifices in supporting my calling to proclaim God's Word. I am so grateful to each of my five children, as I am to my wife, Sarah. Our children can certainly spot both good and bad preaching, and they all look forward to preaching they can really feed on. Sarah's prayers and love for me are an unfailing encouragement, and to her I give this book, with love.

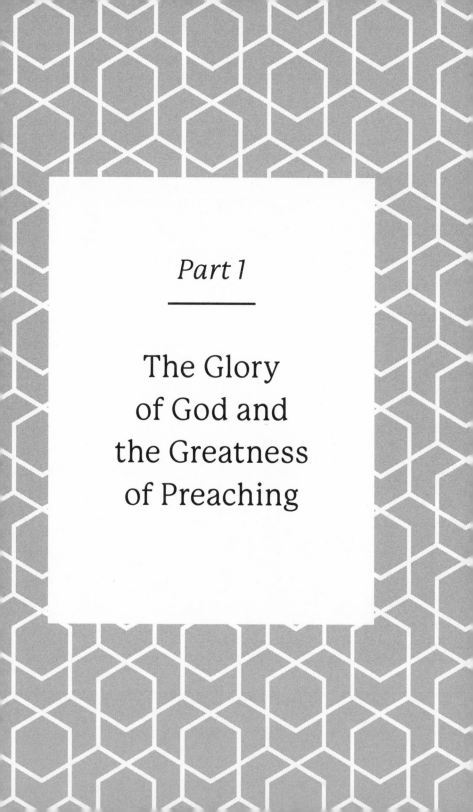

Part 1

———

The Glory of God and the Greatness of Preaching

1

Preaching, above All

Q. What is God's chief end in preaching?
A. God's chief end in preaching is to glorify his name.

The LORD passed before him and proclaimed, "The LORD, the LORD, a God merciful and gracious, slow to anger, and abounding in steadfast love and faithfulness."

Exodus 34:6

Above everything else, those of us who are called to preach need to know that God is love (1 John 4:8). The church's great news to a dying world is that there is a living God, whose love for his creation is inexhaustible. Could we ever love and serve anyone else before him?

Without this conviction our preaching will shrivel and die, and we preachers will soon go the same way. With it, we can believe and do all things. The church has no other and no better message. This is her great declaration.

"God is love" is actually not the same as "God is loving" or "God shows love," though both of these are, of course, true. A God who is loving might be a God who decides to be loving only at times, but no more. The same would be true of a God who shows love. The apostle John means neither. What he is saying in 1 John 4:8 is far bigger and far more exciting. God loves, and shows that love, because he *is* love. Love is of God's essence. And so the source of all reality is a God of ardent, consuming, and delighting love. This is who he is.

Can we speak too much of God's love, though? We all know how the love of God has been pitted against the other divine attributes, as if it somehow neutralizes them. On the one side, there are those who feel that the doctrine of God's love, unless given a myriad of qualifications, might lead to theological liberalism. On the other, the voices insisting that "love wins" effectively state that everything else loses. God's justice, holiness, and sovereignty have all been made to bow to love, as if God's love somehow triumphs over them. Thankfully, such views are wrong. God's love neither conquers nor is crushed by the other attributes. Each exists maximally in the Godhead, for his glory and our good. Let God be a lover, and every man a liar.

God's attributes are never to be viewed as in some sort of tension with each other. We are never in danger of seeing God as being, for example, too sovereign, any more than we might see him as being too merciful or too holy. That is not biblical thinking. God is holy, merciful, sovereign, and loving. He is each one, utterly and completely. He is all of his attributes in their fullest expression, all at the same time. Our preaching about God, as we explore one of his attributes, never needs qualifying or rebalancing by talking about another attribute. Preaching is declaring all that God is.

And God is a preacher. He declares himself the loving Lord. He commanded creation into existence and upholds it all by his Word. His Word governs the planets, and he speaks to our consciences. In his book, the Bible, he shows us what he is like and how we should live. He preaches, in other words. He preaches all the time.

God speaks many words, but he has only one ultimate purpose in the world. As our catechism says, "God's chief end in preaching is to glorify his name." He draws people to discover delight in his Son, Jesus Christ. That is the delight the Father has. He says of his Son,

> Behold my servant, whom I uphold,
>   my chosen, in whom my soul delights;
> I have put my Spirit upon him;
>   he will bring forth justice to the nations. (Isa. 42:1)

Those words are echoed at Christ's baptism and transfiguration, when the voice from heaven says, "This is my beloved Son, with whom I am well pleased; listen to him" (Matt. 3:17; 17:5). "The infinite happiness of the Father," said Jonathan Edwards, "consists in the enjoyment of his Son."[1] Our infinite happiness, as saved sinners, consists in enjoying the Son of God. Delight in Jesus is distinctly godlike, and is God's redemption purpose for the world. The Father is redeeming sinners to be delighters in his Son.

Our salvation involves experiencing the love of the Father, Son, and Spirit. Moments before Jesus was arrested in Gethsemane, he spoke to the Father in prayer: "I made known to them your name, and I will continue to make it known, that the love with which you have loved me may be in them, and I in them" (John 17:26). Knowing Jesus also means knowing the Father.

The God who is, is triune. The Trinity is the revelation of the God who is love. The persons of the Trinity love one another. Delight and mutual honor characterize the persons. The never-lonely, never-needy, majestic and holy God is triune love.

Delighting, serving, being contented, and sharing all things are basic to all authentic love. We long for this sort of commitment and this sort of contentment. Our hearts were created for it, and we know it as love. Augustine said: "Love is the delight of the lover in his beloved. Love's heartbeat is its delight in something else."[2]

---

1. Cited in Steven M. Studebaker and Robert W. Caldwell III, *The Trinitarian Theology of Jonathan Edwards: Text, Context, and Application* (London: Routledge, 2012), 27.

2. Cited in John Owen, *The Works of John Owen*, ed. William H. Goold, vol. 2, *On Communion with God* (Edinburgh: Banner of Truth, 1968), 25n (my translation from the Latin).

The "something else" for each person of the Trinity is the other two persons. Our salvation involves the outreaching of that triune love to bring us into this eternally loving life. Christian discipleship and Christian ministry are life lived in Jesus. Mike Reeves comments:

> We not only come to share the Father's pleasure in him [Christ]; we come to share the life he enjoys before the Father. We stand in him with his own unspotted confidence before his Father—and there the Spirit draws us to live out his life and sonship. That is why he lived and died in our place, that we might live (and die) in his.[3]

What is your heartbeat? Do you love to preach, or do you love the One you preach? Do you love to prep your sermons, enjoying the hard mental and spiritual work, or do you love the One you are discovering more about? As Sunday comes, do you long to lift up the name of the triune God in your preaching, declaring the wonder of the three persons, or is your heart set on getting a bit more congregational love in your direction?

Our challenge as preachers is to remain lovers, to refuse to let our calling, however important and exciting, obscure our primary calling to be captivated ourselves by God's love in Jesus Christ. We must teach others that God is love, and that life on earth is an invitation from heaven to know that love and to live in the light of it. Sermons that are mere information downloads are dry discourses and make for dry Christians, if Christians at all. Rather, we preach so that our hearers discover that the God of love has come to meet them in his Son.

You can only preach what you love. You can only truly love if you know and are daily fed by the love of God. God is always preaching himself, as the God of love. He has no greater message, no other gospel, and no greater purpose. Neither do we.

---

3. Michael Reeves, *Christ Our Life* (Milton Keynes: Paternoster, 2014), 76.

2

Enjoying God

Q. How do we enjoy God?
A. We enjoy God as we submit our hearts to all that he tells us.

—————

With joy you will draw water from the wells of salvation.
Isaiah 12:3

God loves a cheerful preacher. Our ever-blessed, ever-joyful God wants to be proclaimed by those who are brimful of the joy his grace in Christ brings. He calls us to delight in him and, out of that joy, to call others to the feast. Preacher and sermon must be filled with gospel joy. "With joy you will draw water from the wells of salvation" (Isa. 12:3). Preachers who taste, teach, and share the joy of the gospel are truly fulfilling their calling as they serve those who listen.

What I've just said causes some to smart. Life can be so hard, and surely joy is just one of our experiences among the whole range of what we encounter. What about the tears, the heartaches—for some, the months and even years of numbing grief or debilitating illness? It's true, we preachers are often deeply sad—just as everyone else can be. So, why single out joy when joy is so often crowded out by almost anything else?

The reason is that joy, like nothing else, shows whether we really believe the gospel. Joy is gospel authenticity. Joy is not an emotional buzz, an escape from the difficulties we face. To know Jesus Christ means to taste, and to want to taste more, the delights of peace with God the Father, who cares for and smiles on us, the Son, who journeys with us, and the Spirit, who empowers us. Crushingly hard days come, and conscious fellowship with God may be overshadowed for a season; but the triune God is with us. He is our joy.

Joy in Christ and his grace is the most convincing sign that the gospel has won our hearts. If we say we've been brought to Jesus and are his willing servants but live joyless lives, then there is a problem. If we preach out of a heavy sense of obligation, we are in trouble. And if we honestly believe that people will be won for Christ through our dutiful, even faithful and conscientious—but actually joyless— preaching, then we are deceiving ourselves. The whole world is looking for joy. The church is looking for it, too. And everyone's looking at you. You're the preacher, who's supposed to have a message, even a life-transforming one. Are you being changed, then, in this one area that everyone longs for most of all? Are you a joyful preacher, whose words match the revolution you're experiencing?

The men who framed the Westminster Shorter Catechism knew that we are redeemed in Christ to know the joy of God's love. That is life's purpose. As they put it, "Man's chief end is to glorify God, and to enjoy him forever."[1] Life in Christ is not, above all, a set of commands to obey externally but the inward work of the Holy Spirit to remake our minds and hearts. Only then does faith express itself in glad obedience. As those who are led by the Spirit, we are to be led into a life of deepening and joy-filled contentment in Christ.

The Christian life begins with hearing the Word of God in the power of the Spirit and responding to Jesus Christ in repentance

---

1. Answer to Q. 1 in *The Westminster Shorter Catechism* (Edinburgh: Banner of Truth, 2015), 5.

and faith. Christian maturity is an ongoing experience of the same: we see Christ in his Word, and we worship him, gladly giving our hearts to his lordship. We repent of the ways in which we deny his rule of grace over our lives, and we recommit ourselves to him.

The discovery our astonished hearts make as we live the Christian life is that discipleship is an invitation to taste joy. Jesus gives his disciples the promise, "You will know the truth, and the truth will set you free" (John 8:32). That first step with Christ is a step into understanding, reality, truth, and freedom. All the world is looking for those things but failing, as we once were. Now we've been brought by grace to encounter them all in a person, Jesus Christ. Sin once controlled our hearts, but the invasion of God's forgiveness has brought us into a new life of forgiveness and peace. And joy. Joy is offered to us in Jesus (John 15:11; 16:24). Those of us who preach must be eagerly seeking out joy in Christ.

True joy in Christ has many distractions and opponents. One of its greatest opponents is ministry. At times in my own ministry, my heart has felt like a wind tunnel, with prayers and sermon prep all focused on the needs of others rushing through it, while I was struggling to give enough time to ministering to my own spiritual needs. Sunday and midweek deadlines may focus the mind and will, but they can also be the slow (and stressful) death of even the keenest preacher. Jesus ceases to be the delight we're knowing and commending to others and becomes the one whose sweetness has faded. Preaching his Word is no longer the overflowing of joy-captured hearts. If that is the situation we've fallen into, we need to take time out, and begin over again.

So what do we do? We need to give our hearts time and space, and bring them, distraction free, back to the gospel. We need a fresh discovery of just how loved we are in Christ. In life's busyness we need to fight for the time to listen to God's Word. If we don't, the thistles and thorns of work, ministry, and worry will choke our souls. Our hearts need time—time for the Word. We must pray, sing, and worship. Joy-crushing sins and patterns of ungodly behavior must be identified and confessed. There are the many, many blessings that unmerited grace has brought us to reflect on and much joy to be found in our Savior. "Joy in God is a duty of great consequence in the Christian life; and Christians need to be again and again called to it," wrote Matthew Henry.[2] God designs that his church be served by Word-soaked, joy-seeking, and joy-sharing preachers of his delightful gospel. He purposes that those same preachers be mastered by his Word, preaching out of experience.

For that to become reality, the sermon prep will have to wait, and some areas of our lives need a careful and principled neglect. The lawn can grow long, and the bike can rust a little. There are wells of salvation to draw from, and our joy in Christ is at stake. This heart work (as the Puritans would call it) is not an extra duty to add to the many in your busy life. It is the preacher's first responsibility, and not an optional extra.

Martin Bucer, friend and mentor to John Calvin, gave this counsel to ministers of the Word:

> The health and life of the inner man consists in a true living faith in the mercy of God and a sure confidence in the forgiveness of sins which Christ the Lord has acquired and earned for us. This faith and confidence make us truly love God and everything which pleases Him, and bring us his good Spirit, who effects in us a right will and ability to avoid everything that is evil and to do everything that is good.[3]

Good advice. Our crowded age needs to rediscover the wonder of going to God empty-handed but with expectant hearts. Before we would dare to preach his Word, we must ask him to preach it to us, for our growing delight in his Word. "Our joy in the word is the litmus test of the value we actually place on that word."[4]

---

2. Matthew Henry, *Commentary on the Whole Bible*, 6 vols. (Peabody, MA: Hendrickson, 1991), 6:599.

3. Martin Bucer, *Concerning the True Care of Souls* (Edinburgh: Banner of Truth, 2008), 103–4.

4. Christopher Ash, *Bible Delight: Heartbeat of the Word of God* (Fearn, Ross-shire: Christian Focus, 2008), 191.

3

The One We Preach

Q. Who is God?
A. God is the one who perfectly lives, rules, loves, and speaks, all to his own glory.

———

Oh, the depth of the riches and wisdom and knowledge of God! How unsearchable are his judgments and how inscrutable his ways!

> "For who has known the mind of the Lord,
>   or who has been his counselor?"
> "Or who has given a gift to him
>   that he might be repaid?"

For from him and through him and to him are all things. To him be glory forever. Amen.
Romans 11:33–36

Preachers have a single calling, to express who and what God is. This is our mandate, to declare what God has revealed about himself. What could be a greater task than being called to preach God?

So who is God? Define God. Or try to. A growing acquaintance with our Bibles makes us ready to offer our opinions. For those of us familiar with church and ministry, answers rush into our minds and out of our mouths. Wisdom pauses, though. Words matter, and definitions are vital when we talk about God. The more we know about God, and claim to know him, the more we will use our words with care, especially when we're using them about him.

When the men who met at Westminster considered question 4, "What is God?" they struggled to state their answer. The story goes that the debate went back and forth as to how they should define the God of Scripture. No form of words satisfied them, so prayer was called for. One man was asked to pray and so pleaded with God for help. As they prayed with him, all present knew that the words he used must became the catechism's answer to the question. Those words have become a classic expression of what all Christians must believe about God: "God is a spirit, infinite, eternal and unchangeable in his being, wisdom, power, holiness, justice, goodness and truth."[1]

Reread that sentence, and then read it once more. Turn those words over in your mind and feel their truth in your soul. This is your God. He is the great reality who gives all things their meaning. He is the Life all people blindly grope after while instead trying to content themselves with substitute life in success and pleasure. He is the power to which the most jaw-dropping displays of power in nature can only begin to point us. In a world where we are used to being disappointed and lied to, he is the source of all satisfaction and truth. We preachers are to be proclaimers of the truth that is found in God.

And it gets better. Not that God could be more perfect (a blessed impossibility), but that he is seen to be a God of perfect relationships. He is Trinity.[2] God has revealed himself to be three

---

1. George Gillespie (1613–1648), Scottish Puritan pastor, well known for his ministry and godliness, gave voice to these words.
2. Most of our historic confessions treat the being of God first, and afterward explore the Trinity. Are they wrong to do so, given that the Trinity is essential to who God is? I don't think so: God revealed his triune nature only very gradually, mostly through be glimpses

persons. The Father is that reality whose existence proclaims that this world is not an illusion, or a nightmare, or a chaotic mess, but the work of a loving and all-wise God. The Son is the Life, so loving his Father and all that the Father has given him that he came to bring eternal life to all who would place their trust in him. And the power of God is seen in the Spirit, whose power must work to turn hard-hearted and sin-deadened rebels into children of God through the new birth.

The work of the pulpit is to explain to people that the triune God has no needs, least of all a need for the love of his creatures. God is love, and so the Trinity is love—love expressed, received, and delighted in among three persons. The preacher must tell his hearers that God doesn't need any of us, though we assume he does. Instead, the gospel is love, offered to all who seek the embrace of the ever-loving and already-loving God.

The preacher must teach people of God so that they can worship him with all their might. He must preach God so that they learn to adore the God who loves lost people because he chooses to, with no compulsion whatsoever, except the compulsion of the overflowing love of the Trinity. To know this God in his love in Christ is eternal life. The preacher's task is to show them nothing less. Sunday by Sunday, our work must show our hearers that God is the one who lives, rules, loves, and speaks, all to his own glory.

We should never be so foolish as to wonder whether we should preach the gospel or instead teach the Trinity. The God of the gospel is the Trinity. The gospel message is a call to know God in his triune love, both now by faith and one day in eternity with sight and unbreakable joy. God has given the light of the knowledge of his triune glory in the face of Christ (2 Cor. 4:6). Preach the gospel, and you are preaching Trinity love.

The apostle Paul was a man of words, and grace made him a man of worship. Having declared to the Romans the love and

---

and allusions right through the old covenant. Only through the coming of Christ is his tri-unity fully revealed.

work of the Trinity in salvation through Jesus Christ, Paul pauses for breath, and opens his heart in praise:

> Oh, the depth of the riches and wisdom and knowledge of God! How unsearchable are his judgments and how inscrutable his ways!
>
>> "For who has known the mind of the Lord,
>>   or who has been his counselor?"
>> "Or who has given a gift to him
>>   that he might be repaid?"
>
> For from him and through him and to him are all things. To him be glory forever. Amen. (Rom. 11:33–36)

He is glorious. This is the God the Scriptures declare to us (and sing of to us, warn us about, and command us to come to, and urge us to delight in). There can never be a greater hope for the world than to know this God. He is waiting for us.

4

By the Book

Q. What do the Scriptures primarily teach?
A. The Scriptures are all about Jesus, the one to be proclaimed, trusted, and praised.

———

The Scriptures . . . bear witness about me.
John 5:39

My predecessor in my pastorate in London served the church for fifty-one years. One day toward the end of his ministry, a lady asked him, "Won't you ever dry up?" That was a good and an honest question. She wasn't frustrated at his seemingly endless ministry, but she was amazed that he could keep preaching from the same book, week in, week out. The honest answer is that every preacher has dry seasons when his soul or his preaching is shriveled (usually both together). These must be the exceptions, though. And they must be the exceptions because of the book God has given to the preacher for his and his hearers' good. The

Bible is an inexhaustible source of delight, hope, assurance, and compulsion. I discovered this in my first months as a Christian in my late teens. I knew then that if God called me to preaching ministry, I could never get to an end of preaching, and that when all was done, I had only really just started.

Why is the Bible such a thrilling and powerful book? Simply because it is all about Jesus Christ. We might say that the Bible is Jesus's autobiography. This book is his book. Genesis to Revelation are sixty-six mirrors, held up by the Spirit of God so that you and I might see Jesus in his excellence.

We struggle to see Jesus, though. Our eyes are not accustomed to looking for Jesus in whole swathes of the Old Testament. Even when we get to the New Testament, we end up making our Bible reading (and sometimes our sermons) all about ourselves. We forget Jesus as we handle his Word, or we make Jesus the supporting actor as we try to play the lead role in God's drama. No wonder the Bible is a dull book, when we forget that Jesus is its center. It was never actually about us in the first place (nor is it an interesting miscellany of facts, rules, ideologies, or life tips). The Bible is Jesus's book, all that God has to show us about his Son, and all that we need to come to his Son and to be transformed by him. Make the Bible anything less than the discovery of Jesus, and no wonder we can so easily be dull preachers and disciples.

Jesus rebuked his enemies for not realizing that the Bible was all about him (John 5:39–40). He did the same to his disciples (Luke 24:25–27). As my eighteen-year-old son said to me last night, with the confidence and off-hand directness so effortless for teenagers, "Jesus *is* the Bible." I've never put it like that, and that statement needs some qualification, but I quite like it.

When Jesus spoke about the Bible and his central place in it, his words sent shock and delight through his hearers. From his earliest sermons right through to his last, Jesus expounded his place in God's plans and God's Word. For his troubles, Jesus received death-threats, and then a death sentence (see Matt. 26:62–68;

Mark 12:1–12; Luke 4:14–29; John 8:48–59). What Jesus's enemies refused to see, his disciples finally realized, slow though they were, just like us.

The Emmaus road (Luke 24:13–49) is a path worn nearly smooth by the tread of preachers over the centuries. But however many sermons we've heard or even preached on it, its message is still startling and compelling. Luke masterfully retells Jesus's strange appearance to those brokenhearted disciples. Because we readers know that Christ is risen, we can't really enter the despair of the disciples. But listen to the dejection of their hearts: "we had hoped" (v. 21). All their hopes in the Messiah were now broken. Maybe that was once our despair, and it's certainly the quiet despair of many people.

Jesus's way of comfort came through rebuke (vv. 25–26). The disciples misunderstood the cross and doubted the empty tomb. That was because they didn't understand the Scriptures and were lacking in faith. Where their hearts should have been burning at the message of a crucified and risen Messiah, they were instead numb with grief. The risen Christ needed to teach them his gospel, and with that instruction all became clear.

The risen Lord still brings the same transformation. The men on the road had just left Jerusalem, but soon they were coming back to it in the evening. They were willing to take to the road, even at night. That morning they had been brokenhearted, but in the evening they returned with burning hearts (v. 32) to be committed messengers of the risen Christ, the Christ of all the Scriptures.

The point of the narrative for us today is that if we want to see the glory of Christ, we must go to his Word. The Emmaus story ends with Christ disappearing—but his Word remains. He makes himself known through the Scriptures. No other means will tell us about the truth of Christ.[1]

1. I am grateful to my friend Tim Chester for some of my thoughts about the Emmaus episode, which were stimulated by a sermon he preached to church planters in Yorkshire in 2016.

Our job as disciples who are also preachers is to discover that Jesus is at the heart of all Scripture. When we make that personal discovery, then our hearts will start to glow; and once they glow, they will soon start to burn. We want to trust Jesus Christ, giving all that we are to all that he is in his gospel love. We want to praise him as the Lord of all glory, who suffered the pains of hell in our place at the cross. Our calling as disciples is to guard our burning hearts with the help of the Holy Spirit. Our calling as preachers is to get that fire started in the hearts of those we preach to, as trust in him and praise for him are expressed in proclaiming him. As long as we are bringing Christ in all the Scriptures in the power of the Spirit, then we will not fail. That is what we turn to next.

5

Preaching Christ

Q. What is preaching?
A. Preaching is declaring God's truth in Jesus, to the praise of his name.

_____

This grace was given, to preach to the Gentiles the unsearchable riches of Christ.

Ephesians 3:8

What is preaching? Peter Adam defines it as "the explanation and application of the word in the assembled congregation of Christ."[1] God's truth is declared by the preacher, and its meaning is brought home to those who listen. Preaching, though, is ultimately divine activity. J. I. Packer says that it is "the event of God himself bringing to an audience a Bible-based, Christ-related, life-impacting message of instruction and direction through the words

---

1. Peter Adam, *Speaking God's Words: A Practical Theology of Preaching* (Nottingham: Inter-Varsity Press, 1996), 61.

of a spokesperson."[2] If this is preaching, then just how important is it? William Greenhill answers, "Where the word of God is not expounded, preached and applied to the several conditions of the people, there they perish."[3]

The Puritan John Flavel, tireless (and fearless) servant of Jesus Christ, insisted that the only preaching which would do him good must be "hissing hot."[4] He didn't mean he wanted a noisy or showy man in the pulpit, but one who was utterly committed to showing from the Word who Jesus is and why he is therefore so gloriously all-important. Only that sort of preaching brings light and life.

The Emmaus road gives us a vital principle (Luke 24:25–27, 45): hearts that hear Christ in his Word and are opened to him are burning hearts. Those which hear just the Bible, however interesting or even moving the exposition may be, soon grow cold.

So how do we preachers handle the Bible faithfully and accurately so that Jesus is seen in every passage? After all, many passages of Scripture (and probably most) have no evident reference to Jesus, and the connections we preachers try to make can sound forced and leave our listeners maybe rightly unconvinced. How do we preach Christ from every Scripture so that we are not misinterpreting parts of the Bible, or leaving our hearers in a muddle?

Preachers know that this is a vast area of debate, and different opinions set as hard and as fast as concrete on the subject of preaching Christ from all the Scriptures. My own conviction is that we need to be sensitive to what the text is saying in its context, and then fully alive to the progress of redemptive history in which that text (and context) finds its place.

Take a sermon on Judges 3, where Ehud slays the Moab king Eglon and thereby frees God's people from slavery. The preacher will speak of the courage of God's rescuer, an unlikely outsider

---

2. J. I. Packer, "Some Perspectives on Preaching," in *Preaching the Living Word*, ed. David Jackman (Fearn, Ross-shire: Christian Focus, 1999), 28.

3. William Greenhill, quoted in Chad B. Van Dixhoorn, *Confessing the Faith: A Reader's Guide to the Westminster Confession of Faith* (Edinburgh: Banner of Truth, 2014), 187.

4. John Flavel, *Husbandry Spiritualiz'd: Or, The Heavenly Use of Earthly Things* (London, 1765), 27.

called to deliver, and the new chapter of freedom for a rebellious people who follow him. Judges is preoccupied with the themes of God's grace to rebels through the provision of leaders, weak though those leaders often were. Those leaders, including Ehud, are marked by many sins, including pride, cowardice, unbelief, and lack of wisdom. In their best moments as well as their worst, they make us think of a strong leader, though a seemingly unlikely one, who risked his life—and gave it up at the cross—defeating sin and the Evil One, and bringing freedom to repentant and trusting captives.

Is that too easy an example? (Forgive me; I just heard a great sermon on it preached by my colleague.) So, what about the passages that don't seem to explore the dominant Bible themes of sin and redemption? Where is Jesus, say, in the protracted romance of Jacob and Rachel, or in the portioning of the land to the Israelite tribes under Joshua, or in the terrible personal conflicts of the prophets, or in the tears of the widows of Elijah and Elisha's day? And how can we speak of Jesus when we read of the temple pillars' pomegranates?

In all these places and ten thousand more, Jesus speaks, and he speaks of himself. He speaks through those frustrated hearts and assigned acres and worship artifacts, and they all lead us to him as we understand that the Bible has one plotline, and that every detail—every one—leads us on in the unfolding of that plot. As Sinclair Ferguson says, "From Genesis 3:15 to the end, the Bible is the story of God the Warrior coming to the aid of His people in order to deliver them from the kingdom of darkness and to establish his reign among, in and through them."[5] So wherever you see tears, beauty, riches, or worship in the Bible, you are seeing glimpses of the One in whom all these things find their ultimate value and significance.

Let this sink in, and let it shape your Bible reading and your preaching ministry. No text is ever properly handled if people

---

5. Sinclair B. Ferguson, *Preaching Christ from the Old Testament* (London: The Proclamation Trust, 2002), 8.

aren't led into its truth that Jesus is center-stage in God's drama. We must therefore read Scripture expecting to see him, his unfolding victory, and his tender grace on all its pages.

When we preach, it is to those who are mostly weary, tempted, and weak in faith. We teach them, but we aim to do more than that. We aim to see their hearts comforted by the truth we teach them. Therefore we prepare, pray over, and then declare the truth as it is found in Jesus in order to call our hearers to give themselves to Jesus with renewed hope. The preacher breaks the bread in such a way that the church feeds on Christ from every Scripture.

John Newton wrote to a friend to encourage him in his Christian walk. Of Jesus Christ he said,

> To view him by faith, as living, dying, reigning, interceding and governing for us, will furnish us with such views, prospects, motives, and encouragements, as will enable us to endure any cross, to overcome all opposition, to withstand temptation, and to run in the way of his commandments with an enlarged heart.[6]

This is what we are doing in our preaching. Preaching knows no greater goal, and allows no lesser one.

---

6. Quoted in Tony Reinke, *Newton on the Christian Life: To Live Is Christ* (Wheaton, IL: Crossway, 2015), 270.

6

All Our Days

Q. What is the preacher's chief end?
A. The chief end of the preacher is to glorify God and to enjoy him forever.

———

Lift up your hands to the holy place
and bless the LORD!
Psalm 134:2

Every preacher is a lover. We have big hearts, big dreams, and big desires. But the preacher's greatest loves may be his greatest dangers. If we are going to immerse ourselves in this precarious business of preaching, we need to get clear, as soon as we can, why we're doing it. Failure to do this will definitely risk failure in our work.

Some loves are obviously sinful for the preacher. We might love approval and the praise others give us. We might love the power we believe we have over people as we speak and they listen (or at least they appear to). We might love the chance to impress with our learning and our skill in using words. We might love the study we put into our preparation, regardless of whether our preaching helps the listeners or not. Preaching can be so very gratifying, even when there's little sign of grace at work.

Do you love to preach? The fact that you're reading this book suggests you do. Why do you love to preach, though?

Psalm 134 is the second shortest of the 150, having just three verses. But it packs a massive and surprising punch for every servant of God. Here we are challenged to find our hearts' rest in the love of God, even when life is at its most humdrum. And we preachers are called, for the most part, to humdrum lives.

The psalm is the last of the collection known as the Psalms of Ascent. These are fifteen songs for God's people seeking to walk with God. For Israel, that meant songs for the three-times-a-year journeys to worship in Jerusalem, and for Christians today, the whole life of journeying by faith. In Psalm 134 the Jerusalem pilgrims are most likely setting off, perhaps before sunrise, back to their homes in Israel. They give a last thought to the priests in the temple,

> you servants of the LORD,
>> who stand by night in the house of the LORD. (v. 1)

Their work, even in the dwelling place of the Almighty, was nonetheless pretty unexciting, especially at night, when they would have been working effectively as security guards and cleaners. And at night no one would have seen them to acknowledge their work with thanks. It was tiring and tedious, and came with very few earthly rewards.

Unexciting, unseen, and unappreciated. Maybe the priest thought he was called to so much more. Most preachers do. We want response, growth, revival, and maybe plenty of affirmation along the way. Some preachers do get that. But they are the exceptions, and we need to know it.

Most of us are working the night shift. To be sure, preaching is often a thrilling business. People are won to Christ through our ministry, believers mature through the preached Word, problems are dealt with as people understand Bible preaching and apply it to their lives, and individuals are slowly shaped together into authentic Christian communities. There are times when glory breaks in and God is powerfully present and at work among his people. Most of our work, though, is torchlight work, carried out in the often dim light of faith.

The work is slow, and progress is usually the fruit of preaching week in, week out, and decade upon decade. Our labors are often unrecognized, and the demands of this mostly unseen and often unappreciated work take their toll on preachers and their families. When results are few and the costs are high, every preacher needs to ask himself regularly, why am I doing this?

Allow that fleeting temple scene in the psalm to reach you. The pilgrims encourage the priests not to lose heart:

> Lift up your hands to the holy place
>   and bless the LORD! (v. 2)

Worship him, in other words, when no one notices you and when the work is unexciting. Remember in those times that God loves you; he sees you and honors all your labors. Remember that in due season you will receive your reward if you don't give up (Gal. 6:9). Self-pity is as much out of place in Christian ministry as self-promotion is. Worship him because of who he is, the Lord of heaven and earth.

You're preaching for God. You're preaching because he has been pleased to call and equip you to preach, and he is pleased as you preach. If he ordains that you find the tasks of preparing and delivering your sermon enjoyable, then he gets the glory. If he makes your preaching obviously fruitful, again, it's for his name's sake. But if you preach only because you enjoy it, or even because people seem to value it, then you are in trouble. The minute those things vanish, your heart will be laid bare, and you will see yourself (maybe others will, too), for what you were all along—

a preacher more taken up with his own desires than with the glory of God.

The life of a Christian, and of a Christian preacher, is a moment-by-moment giving of all his heart to God and God's grace, in the power of the Holy Spirit. Keep your heart—or even a piece of it—for yourself, and you are in great trouble. James K. A. Smith explains: "Our hearts . . . are like existential compasses and embodied homing beacons: our loves are pulled magnetically to some north toward which our hearts have been calibrated. Our actions and behavior—indeed, a whole way of live—are pulled out of us by this attraction to some vision of the good life."[1]

This is our daily fight, and this is where the path to joyful service lies. Get your heart pulled in its deepest impulses to God in Jesus Christ, and your preaching ministry, however difficult, will be a fitting expression of your life's worship.

---

1. James K. A. Smith, *You Are What You Love* (Grand Rapids, MI: Brazos, 2016), 57.

7

Confident of This

Q. How can we rest in God's power and purposes?
A. We are confident that God is in charge and at work through the joys and sometimes failures of preaching.

———

He sleeps and rises night and day, and the seed sprouts and grows; he knows not how.
Mark 4:27

God is building a kingdom through his Son and throughout the world. The kingdom is established by the preached Word. The parable of the farmer and the soils in Mark 4:1–20 is Jesus's definitive guide to what his work is, and what ours is if we heed his call to declare the Word. As the kingdom grows, there will be opposition (including from Satan), indifference, promising starts that lead to crushing disappointment, misunderstanding, and also astonishing growth. We have been warned and inspired.

Young preachers soon discover that the words of Jesus are true. We see revolutions in people's lives as God's power is unleashed through the ministry of his Word, but we also see the letting loose of all manner of unexpected and discouraging reactions to ministry. Preaching looks, to all the world and sometimes to the church, like an easy ticket. Those who feel the weight of God's call know that in fact it is hard work.

In the last sermon he ever prepared for a pastors' gathering (he actually died before he delivered it), John Flavel warned his fellow laborers of this. Quoting Martin Luther, he said:

> "The labours of the ministry will exhaust the very marrow from your bones, hasten old age and death" (Luther). They are fittingly compared to the toil of men in harvest, to the labours of a woman in travail, and to the agonies of soldiers in the dangers of battle. We must watch when others sleep.
>
> It is not so much the expense of our labours, as the loss of them, that kills us. It is not with us, as with other labourers. They find their work as they leave it, not so with us. Sin and Satan unravel almost all we do, the impressions we make on our people's souls in one sermon, vanish before the next. How many truths have we to study! How many strategies of Satan, and mysteries of corruption, to detect! How many cases of conscience to resolve! We must fight in defence of the truths we preach, as well as study them to paleness, and preach them unto faintness. But well-spent head, heart, lungs, and all; welcome pained breasts, aching backs, and trembling legs, if we can by all but approve ourselves Christ's faithful servants, and hear that joyful voice from his mouth, "Well done, good and faithful servants."[1]

Flavel was right. There are costs to be faced up to in a preaching ministry. Preaching is tiring, often discouraging, and the focus of Satan's attacks. The preacher must deal with deep subjects in a way that is plain and helpful. None of this is easy. Preachers quickly need to find perspective and motivation to keep them at the task.

---

1. John Flavel, *The Character of a True Evangelical Pastor, Drawn by Christ*, in *The Works of John Flavel*, 6 vols. (Edinburgh: Banner of Truth, 1968), 6:569.

One of my favorite Bible passages in this regard is the one that follows the parable of the farmer and the soils in Mark 4:1–9 and takes its meaning further (Mark 4:26–29). Jesus says of the sown word, "The earth produces by itself, first the blade, then the ear, then the full grain in the ear" (v. 28). The farmer goes tired to his bed. The seed is in the ground. His work looks ordinary, and the next day there will be nothing to show for it. Out of sight, though, something wonderful is happening. The seed will germinate, the stalk will grow, and corn will be ready for the harvest (vv. 27–29).

That is the mystery of preaching. The seed of God's Word is no sooner planted than it is hidden, buried, seemingly forgotten and dead. The preacher does his work, and he goes home. But then the Holy Spirit goes to work. He causes that seed to establish itself in the hearts of hearers. He brings the miracle of faith and life. Our part is significant—faith comes through hearing (Rom. 10:17)—but the Spirit does the life-giving work, and God gets the glory. "So neither he who plants nor he who waters is anything, but only God who gives the growth" (1 Cor. 3:7).

A preacher needs to grow in childlike dependence upon God's grace for himself and for his listeners, year by year. "For we walk by faith, not by sight" (2 Cor. 5:7) should be a verse put in every pastor's study and in every pulpit. The preacher needs plenty of faith, because sight can be so deceptive—and discouraging.

Haven't you noticed how preaching sometimes goes wrong? Congregations don't get the point of the sermon, no matter how hard we've tried to be simple. People take offense when we've had no intention of offending them (the opposite also happens). Those we've prayed and prepared for most carefully in the week aren't there for the sermon. Our best sermons are often our biggest disasters. We go home frustrated, embarrassed, deflated, and wondering what all the effort was for.

Again, faith is needed. Preaching, even preaching that looks like it's crashing and burning, is never a waste in God's purposes (Isa. 55:11). We are not God, and we should gladly admit that we have no idea how he works through our often feeble efforts for his glory. We don't need to know, and we need to stop fretting. God is at work. We believe his promise.

The question we must face, and which our post-sermon activities betray, is this: can we find heart peace as we trust that God is at work? Whether we're jogging off our adrenaline or collapsed on the sofa, is there trust in our hearts? Do we really believe that our preaching will achieve God's work?

Faith is part of our spiritual armor. As we leave our preaching, we must leave both our preaching and our hearers with God. They are all safe with him, and so are we. With the Spirit's gift of faith, after we've done everything, then we can stand (Eph. 6:13).

8

Called to Preach

Q. Why do we believe that God called us to preach?
A. We know that God creates and calls preachers. His Word and our own experience tell us so.

———

I press on toward the goal for the prize of the upward call of God in Christ Jesus.
Philippians 3:14

The language of a "call to preach" is deeply unfashionable today. For a start, doesn't the language of "call" make preachers sound a bit too important when God loves all equally, whether preachers or publicans? We rightly want to affirm the value in God's sight of every calling, from stay-at-home motherhood to high-pressure banking with a long commute thrown in. Why single out preaching ministry as something different that needs a call?

This good question often arises from a darker impulse. If preachers are that important, then maybe we need to listen more

carefully to what they have to say. Our antiauthoritarian age shies
from anything that might suggest trust and obedience. That some
among us—the preachers—believe they are appointed by God to
speak to us all raises our secularized suspicions. But we cannot
shrug off God's will or relativize his servants. He speaks, and he
speaks as appointed men proclaim his Word.

The idea of a call is in the Bible. Every believer is called to
Christ (and called to serve Christ, 1 Cor. 1:9) in a discipleship that
will involve suffering (Mark 8:34–35; 1 Pet. 2:21). "To the fellowship of his ministry Christ calls every Christian,"[1] says Edmund
Clowney. To the call to Christ and the call to serve Christ in every
sphere, add the specific call for some to proclaim his Word. The
church in Acts would publicly recognize men as servants of the
Word whom the Spirit set apart (Acts 13:2–4). Where the church
of Christ has done that through the ages, she has affirmed the call
of God. John Calvin identified the two aspects of a call of God to
ministry: the individual's inner compulsion ("I *have* to do this")
and the church's recognition of the man's necessary godliness and
gifts in handling God's Word.[2]

The Westminster Shorter Catechism teaches us that we are
created in God's image (Q. 10) and that our lives are shaped by
his providence (Q. 11).[3] The call to preach is to bring the truth of
the unseen God to the world, and is confirmed in the way he has
directed our lives and our gifts.

When Is a Call Mistaken?

Before we go further, though, let's clear up three misconceptions
about God's call.

You're not called just because you enjoy preaching. No, you're
not. Enjoying something doesn't mean competence at it. Being

---

1. Edmund P. Clowney, *Called to the Ministry* (Philadelphia: Presbyterian and Reformed, 1964), 42.
2. John Calvin, *Institutes of the Christian Religion*, ed. John T. McNeill, trans. Ford Lewis Battles (London: SCM Press, 1959), 4.3.15.
3. *The Westminster Shorter Catechism* (Edinburgh: Banner of Truth, 2015), 8.

keen on preaching doesn't mean you're called to it. Of course, local churches and their leaders need to recognize and promote the gifting that the Spirit has given to every member of the body of Christ for gospel service (1 Cor. 12:12–31; Eph. 4:11–13). Equally, church leaders and members must not be held to ransom by the mere enthusiasm of any individual to do something—least of all, to preach.

You're not called just because people like your preaching. Affirmation is a precious gift when used in the church, but it can also be a problem. The three people who loved Mr. So-and-so's sermon and told him so may be easily outnumbered by those who suffered it in silence. Mr. So-and-so swells with excitement (and maybe no small pride): "They love me!" Well, they may love him, and a few may have appreciated his preaching. But a call to preach must be confirmed by more than your wife and your two best friends.

You're not even called because you feel compelled to preach. Many evangelical churches have members who are convinced they should be preaching. Some are distinctly "Absalomish," convinced that their gifts are the answer to the church's problems, and that they're the ones to do it where others are failing (see 2 Sam. 15:1–6). If you are called, however, you will know it when your ministry is compelling to others.

When Is a Call Valid?
So how do we identify the call in our lives and seek to respond to it in ways that will be confirmed by others?

You're called when you feel overwhelmed by preaching. Preaching is the most thrilling, glorious, and wonderful calling, and also the most daunting and, at times, terrifying. Church history is full of stories of men who tried to avoid the call of God to preach. The Scottish Reformer John Knox was called to the work of preaching and pastoring in the course of a worship service by a preacher who declared it was God's and the congregation's will. Knox ran out of the gathering in tears and locked himself in his room. Five years before, in Geneva, the young John Calvin had a pretty similar reaction to the call to serve the Lord in the ministry of preaching. And when a friend of mine was asked to preach for the first time in his church, he was so terrified that he frantically looked for any convincing excuse from having to preach—including putting his house on the market so that he could leave the area!

"Who is sufficient for these things?" (2 Cor. 2:16). If we feel that *we* are in ourselves, we probably haven't been preaching for long enough. When it comes to preaching, time is a great breaker of misplaced confidence. The time will come when we are all broken by our failure, our sin, or other people's. Then the Holy Spirit can get to work on us, shaping us to be true, Christlike servants, knowing that our sufficiency comes from God alone. And this he delights to do.

You're called when you have a deep love for those who need God's Word. True preachers love people. They pray for them, listen to them, and serve them, both in and outside the pulpit. They love to be with them. Part of loving people also means a commitment to being apart from them, putting disciplined and often lonely hours into preparing sermons that will show them Christ and help them to grow in a deepening love for him. True preachers are gentle, as the apostle Paul models and commands (1 Thess. 1:6–9; 2 Tim. 2:24–25). And those called are men of prayer, who by their prayers labor in private to serve those to whom they preach. That is a solid act of love.

You're called when you are ready to suffer in the service of God's Word. If you see serving people as a pain and not a privilege, if setting out chairs on a Sunday is something you've "grown out of," if handling painful and unfair criticism for your ministry is a no-no, and if you refuse to be accountable for what you've said in a sermon, then the warning signs are there. God had one Son, and he was a servant. Only the servant-hearted are called to be servants of the Word.

These are the three essential marks of God's call. We must add to them, of course, a gifting for unfolding God's words. But mere gifting is not the call. God creates his servants and calls them to be like Jesus. That calling, given and sealed by the Holy Spirit, leads to a lifetime's fruitful ministry.

9

For God, for People

Q. Why does God call us to preach?
A. God calls us to serve all of our hearers with his gospel.

———

We work with you for your joy, for you stand firm in your faith.
2 Corinthians 1:24

The people who have most influenced you for good in your Christian journey are those who have told you the truth. Whether that's in personal friendship or through pulpit ministry, they've served you with God's wisdom. That will have included hard things, too, things that made you sad or angry (or both), until the Holy Spirit softened your heart and brought repentance, faith, and change. Love speaks the truth.

Love also speaks the truth in the right way. We cannot expect people to know that we love them unless they hear love in our words and see it in our faces. The way we speak is as important as what we say. Both together are the grace of God working through our ministry.

When the truth is spoken in love, God is honored. In fact, such words have God's glory as their aim. There is no tension at all between serving people and honoring God. People are served as God's Word is expounded to them, and God is glorified as his Word is declared. Therefore, preaching that separates the two achieves neither goal. You cannot honor God unless you are ministering the fullness of the gospel with gospel love for the good of the lost and the saved.

Preaching to the glory of God is all about helping others to grasp and delight in the truth of the gospel. God's glory revealed in the cross of Christ and declared in preaching *is* the good of grace-hungry people. "The eternal salvation of the human soul, through the presentation of divine truth, is the end of preaching," William Shedd wrote.[1] That is what God wants from you, and that is what your hearers need from you, regardless of whether they currently understand that or actually want it. Anything less is just bad preaching.

So, preaching is a pursuit of giving glory to God as his gospel truth in Jesus Christ is lovingly declared. As long as he gets the glory, what does it really matter what happens to us? If the splendor of God outshines and outlasts the tiny splendor of a billion suns, does your gratification in ministry really mean anything? Is your reputation of the slightest importance? Of course not. Preaching must always be an exercise in self-effacement, not self-promotion, or even self-fulfillment. Jesus says, "Feed my sheep," not "Feed your ego." People must be led to Christ, and led on with Christ through preaching.

Our call to preach is our ordination to love people by bringing them the Word of God in the power of the Spirit. To do that, we must know those we preach to. That takes commitment. You must open your life to them before you should expect that they'll open their lives to you. Then, as you begin to see their needs, dreams, struggles, and fears, you will go to the Word looking for ways to serve them. John Flavel helps us here:

---

1. William G. T. Shedd, *Homiletics and Pastoral Theology* (Edinburgh: Banner of Truth, 1965), 37.

A prudent minister will study the souls of his people more than the best human books in his library, and not choose what is easiest for him, but what is most necessary for them. Ministers that are acquainted with the state of their flocks, as they ought to be, will be seldom at a loss in the choice of the next subject. Their people's needs will choose their text for them. . . . This will direct us to the great doctrines of conviction, regeneration, and faith, and will make us sit thoughtfully in our studies, asking "Lord, what course shall we take, and what words shall we use that may best convey the sense of their sin and danger, with the fullness and necessity of Christ, to their hearts?"[2]

My favorite text about Christian ministry, bar none, is 2 Corinthians 1:24: "Not that we lord it over your faith, but we work with you for your joy, for you stand firm in your faith." Every part of Paul's declared ministry mandate here is pregnant with significance. It makes sense of his work with the Corinthians and also gives us marching orders for preaching that aims at the glory of God in the service of our hearers. Three great preaching priorities demand attention:

"Not that we lord it over your faith." We are servants of the Word. Servants. Let that word register. Preaching is not about wielding power over others but about becoming a servant. Servants have only one calling, to work for the sake of others. Many in the church at Corinth had grown to mistrust Paul and trust instead in worldly preachers. Some felt that he was domineering. Some in our congregations now suspect that their preachers are in it for what they personally can get out of it. We need to persevere in lovingly serving God's people so that they will have no reason to suspect us. We are earnestly trying to serve their faith in Jesus.

"We work with you for your joy." For your joy! These three words should send shock waves through every preacher. Our goal

---

2. John Flavel, *The Character of a True Evangelical Pastor, Drawn by Christ*, in *The Works of John Flavel*, 6 vols. (Edinburgh: Banner of Truth, 1968), 6:571.

is to deepen the joy of our hearers in Jesus Christ. He is the pearl of great price, the bread of life, the splendor of heaven. Without finding our joy in him, we will shrivel up, just going through the motions as disciples. But if we discover that Jesus is so wonderful and glorious, we will live eagerly and boldly for him. Preaching which honors God and helps people is transparently humble and loving, and builds joy-filled confidence in Christ.

"You stand firm in your faith." Some at Corinth were confident that they were standing firm (1 Cor. 10:12), but they were showing little evidence of grace. Complacency is the Devil's work. Satan tempts all of us to believe that we are safe apart from relying on God's grace alone. Ministry is the battle against mistrust and misapplied confidence, in our own lives as well as in the lives of those we preach to. God will lovingly shake us out of our self-confidence and will use any means to make us look to him and grow in faith. As we grow in faith, we call others to join us in trusting our great example of faith, the Lord Jesus.

God has invested his glory in his children seeing and delighting in the saving grace of his Son in his proclaimed Word. This is the glorious calling we pursue. "Who is sufficient for these things?" (2 Cor. 2:16). By grace, and only by grace, we are.

10

Not a Square Inch

Q. What else did God ordain?
A. God ordained that all things should be preached as being under the headship of Christ.

———

Who then is this, that he commands even winds and water, and they obey him?

Luke 8:25

Those who are called to preach must be sure that God has called everything else into his purposes. It's no good being convinced that the Lord wants you in the pulpit if you're not really sure about his involvement in the world beyond your allotted few square feet of activity each Sunday. Jesus rules from the pulpit, and he also reigns over doing the dishes, health scares, financial markets, and struggling marriages. The people we serve, the mistakes we make, the wins and the losses of ministry, the tragedies and sins we face in our churches and families—these are all equally under his sovereign control. You are preaching into a universe ruled by King Jesus. This life-changing truth must be the solid ground for all your preaching. Believe it, and preach it.

"All authority in heaven and on earth has been given to me," Jesus said (Matt. 28:18). The winds and sea recognized that (Mark 4:39). So did disease, death, the demonic, and heaven itself. It took the disciples far longer to understand. It still does. Our default belief is that God is involved in the brilliant but is far from the tragic. There is more than a little whiff of paganism about that, isn't there? And if we give that conviction any ground, we will be anxious and discouraged preachers.

Yet again, we must preach the gospel to ourselves. The gospel is the declaration that there is a King. All claims to authority in this world that do not acknowledge and submit to the kingship of Jesus are imposters, rebels, and enemies. All fears we may have that our ministry is melting because God isn't really ruling our circumstances are the signs of a dangerous unbelief. We must shock our fears by "saying that there is another king, Jesus" (Acts 17:7). This King is as much for us as he rules in loving and effortless power over us. And so we take heart.

Our calling is to speak gospel words in what often appears to be the chaos of our lives and the lives of our congregations. "Our God reigns" must never sound trite. It must always be heard for what it is, a uniquely hope-filled and peace-bringing claim. Our world is not purposeless, but deep down most of the hearts of those we preach to fear that it is. They look at their own lives, scarred with failure and tragedy, and many are nearly broken with sorrow. How can this mess serve any purpose? How can God be both powerful and good, given the lives believers have to cope with?

We literally cannot survive as Christians without making and believing the confident assertion that Christ is still ruling the winds and the waves. Kevin Vanhoozer says it well: "He is the divine Son in and through whom all things have been made (Col. 1:16) *and remade*—that is, made right and rightly ordered."[1] Although the evidence of our world and the fears of our hearts suggest otherwise, Christ truly "upholds the universe by the word of his power" (Heb. 1:3). Everything is under his command; nothing escapes his lordship.

Believing that Christ is Lord is the work of all of our hearts, for all of our lives. As John Owen explained, "Believing is an act of the heart; which in the Scriptures comprises all the faculties of the soul."[2] Pause and reflect on that: do we preachers really get how demanding and difficult faith is? Yes and no. No, we probably don't, on many levels. The Spirit has gifted us with a confidence in the gospel (however shaky that faith sometimes gets) so that we feel compelled to preach. They won't tell us, but many in our churches would quite frankly feel *I could never do that* as they watch us, because they rightly see that preaching is a business that stretches faith, sometimes to the limit. Preachers are, by most measurements, believers with a good deal of faith. Because of that, it's all too easy to fail to appreciate the struggles many of our hearers have in believing.

There again, time spent with fellow Christians who suffer, or time spent in our own trials, brings home the fact that faith is anything but natural or straightforward. Ours is not a simple or an easy reflex to trust in Jesus when life is horrible, and sometimes even when life is wonderful. Doesn't a glance at your own life as a preacher actually show you how hard you find faith? Our fluctuating moods and occasional spectacular emotional collapses might just be pointers to how hard we find faith to be. We preachers are heavy lifters, bearing our own problems and the difficulties of those we serve through preaching. Faith is hard for us. Our whole souls need to be fixed on Christ.

Faith is a hungry business, and true faith must be continually fed. The undershepherds need a diet of good food just as the sheep do. Key to that diet is a robust confidence in Christ's lordship. We

---

1. Kevin Vanhoozer, *Biblical Authority after Babel: Retrieving the* Solas *in the Spirit of a Mere Protestant Christianity* (Grand Rapids, MI: Brazos, 2016), 90.
2. John Owen, *The Works of John Owen*, ed. William H. Goold, vol. 5, *Faith and Its Evidences* (Edinburgh: Banner of Truth, 1968), 115.

must believe through constant meditation on the Scriptures, and we must make sure that it has a high place in the preaching we bring to those we serve. All things—preachers, disciples, disasters, and joys—really are under his wise and loving command.

> Let not the wise man boast in his wisdom, let not the mighty man boast in his might, let not the rich man boast in his riches, but let him who boasts boast in this, that he understands and knows me, that I am the LORD who practices steadfast love, justice, and righteousness in the earth. For in these things I delight, declares the LORD. (Jer. 9:23–24)

This is true theology, which alone can kindle the fire of faith and devotion.

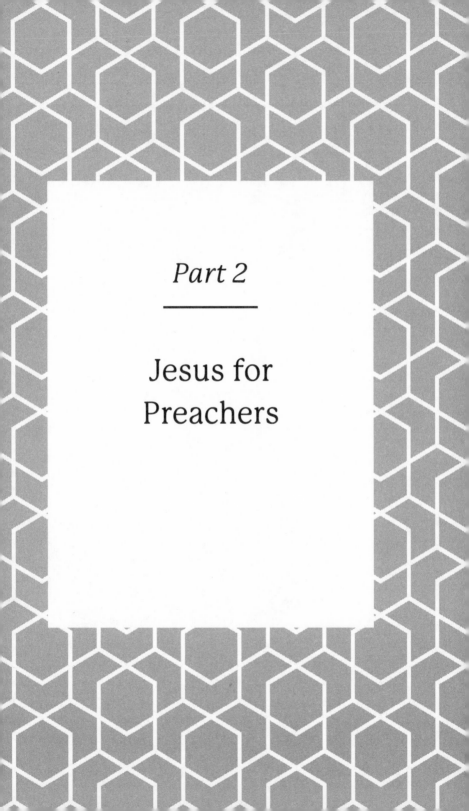

Part 2

———

Jesus for
Preachers

11

Sin

Q. How did the first preacher sin?
A. He took the fruit of preaching and ate it for his own pleasure.

———

Have you eaten of the tree of which I commanded you not to eat?
Genesis 3:11

Adam was called to be a preacher. He was set apart by God in the garden to declare God's truth to creation. He was to serve Eve by bringing God's declared will to her, and together they were to love, serve, and fill God's creation as bearers of his image. They were to steward his will through his word.

They failed, of course. Adam and Eve listened to Satan rather than to God. They looked at the fruitfulness of obedience and exchanged it for the bitter fruit of self-will. The tree of the knowledge of good and evil appeared to promise everything but left them guilty, ashamed, and frightened.

The pulpit is not a place safe from sin. Quite the opposite. All sorts of wickedness arise when men prepare and preach sermons.

And just like the sin of the first couple, so we grab the unlawful fruit of preaching, and it is devastating.

In 1674 the London pastor Thomas Vincent wrote some notes to fill out the Westminster Shorter Catechism's teaching.[1] He details seven ways in which Adam and Eve failed God:

1. Rebellion. They defied the Sovereign Lord.
2. Treason. They sided with the Devil against God.
3. Ambition. They longed to be like God.
4. Luxury. They set their hearts on tasting the fruit.
5. Unbelief. God warned them, but instead they believed the Devil.
6. Ingratitude. They wanted this fruit, and so spurned God's goodness in the gift of the fruit of all of the other trees.
7. Murder. They brought death on themselves, and on all of their posterity.[2]

Hang on, though. Isn't trying to apply this list to our calling as preachers, and pin these sins on ourselves, a little over the top? How many ministers actually preach in order to satisfy the urge for material comforts? Who preaches as an act of rebellion against God? Few of us steal sermons or lust after the women we preach to. Praise God for that. We know the Spirit's leading and empowering for ministry. We are often conscientious, prayerful, and genuinely hard at work to bring glory to God as we proclaim his Word. But who says we're safe or always pure in heart?

All preachers have a deep instinct to beat a path back to that tree, so to speak. Called to obedience, we fantasize about disobedience, and want to chase after it. Called to serve God with our preaching, we so often want to use our ministry to serve ourselves. Called to be preachers of the Word in season and out of season (2 Tim. 4:2), we find that we are fair-weather preachers, faithful when it suits us, faithless when it doesn't. In our sin we take the

---

1. Thomas Vincent, *The Shorter Catechism Explained from Scripture* (Edinburgh: Banner of Truth, 1980).
2. Vincent, *Shorter Catechism Explained*, 58.

Word of God and turn it for our own ends. Deep down we have a longing for control, for comfort, and for approval.

The last Adam was a preacher as fearless as he was sinless. He always spoke God's Word in obedience to his Father and in the service of his listeners. His loyalty to God's Word took him to another tree, the cross, to die there as our Sin-Bearer (1 Pet. 2:24). Even from that tree he preached words of love, praying for his enemies, bringing forgiveness, and commanding love (Luke 23:34, 43; John 19:27). He obeyed where Adam failed and won for all his own the right to the tree of life (Rev. 22:14). We don't just go to him for enabling grace to preach to sinners; we go to him for forgiving grace for our sins as preachers.

There are times when every preacher needs to take stock. How am I preaching? Why am I preaching? And have I degraded the holy ministry of preaching by turning it into an unholy self-service project?

Here a few questions to help us to assess whether sin has crept into our preaching:

1. What happens in my heart when people thank me for my preaching? Do I straight away silently thank God that they were blessed? Or do I thank myself for my skills as a preacher?

2. When I preach a terrible sermon, why does it devastate me? Is it because I don't think that Christ's sheep have been fed? Or is it because my ego hasn't been stroked?

3. Do I preach to serve my hearers or to scratch my own preaching itches? Do I choose passages for the pulpit because I know they will serve where my hearers are in need or because I prefer them and think I preach them well?

4. When someone says something critical that is true but painful about my preaching (to me or to someone else, and it has gotten back to me), is my first response angry self-pity, or do I give God thanks for this Spirit-given opportunity to grow in my preaching?

5. Should I adopt a different preaching tone and style or perhaps preach shorter sermons in order to reach my hearers more effectively? Or do pride and fear tie me to preaching as I always have?

6. Do I ever have the courage to ask those closest to me (my wife or the church's leaders) about my preaching? Am I prepared for honest and loving feedback, or do I wish to keep justifying my ministry exactly as it is?

These are uncomfortable questions. But we need to ask them. In the presence of God, the Holy Spirit assures our broken hearts that we have nothing to fear. May he give us the grace to be truer preachers, for Christ's sake.

12

Weakness

Q. What is the good news for struggling preachers?
A. The gospel is true and always for us, especially on Mondays.

———

But we have this treasure in jars of clay, to show that the surpassing power belongs to God and not to us.

2 Corinthians 4:7

Monday is the preacher's dog day. Ask any of us. In the cold light of day we see just how far short we fell from what we wanted and hoped for. After Sunday's giving of ourselves, now we just want to disappear, weary and (often) fretful. We feel spent—and we are.

We're spent because preaching is totally consuming. It is a delight, but it also brings great danger. Most preachers love their calling. It is a great joy, as well as a daunting responsibility. Many of us who are pastors don't want to think of a retirement without preaching. Nor is that necessarily a cause for concern: for a preacher to delight in his ministry needn't mean that it is his self-justification. The best preachers will happily listen to others in the pulpit. They don't *need* to preach, in the sense that they're justified by preaching. It's just that preaching is the consuming desire of their lives.

People in evangelical churches occasionally catch glimpses of the work and the cost of preaching, and they're almost always surprised and often shocked. "It takes you *how long* to prepare your sermons?" Ask a promising younger man in church if he would consider preaching his first sermon, and his breezy confidence is soon exchanged for a careworn, weight-of-the-world expression as the appointed Sunday comes into view. I know men who've held high-pressure jobs in big business and are now in full-time preaching ministry. They tell me how the responsibilities of handling God's Word bring a unique strain, week in and week out. Perhaps no one realizes what a heavy responsibility the preacher's task is except the man in the pulpit.

My Sundays now are fueled by two things—grace and adrenaline. I wake early on a Sunday with that churning feeling of *why couldn't I be a postman or a marine biologist or just about anything else?* I get to my study early to pray and work through my notes. I preach at church just as well as I'm able to, grace allowing. If I preach again in the evening, I'm frequently left on a high, relieved at the close of another Lord's Day, so grateful for the privilege, cheered by signs of engagement from my hearers, and (usually) eager to start the work of prep all over again for next week.

There's a famous old slogan we preachers love. The American pastor Phillips Brooks famously said, "If any man be called to preach, don't stoop to be a king." I love these words, because I know how they affirm the preacher's task. I passionately believe that preaching is the highest and best calling this side of glory.

So what about our Mondays? Some preachers (and the books they read on preaching) just want to dismiss our Monday collapses. The reasoning goes like this: *You're tired. The Devil's having a go at you. You need to rest anyway. Forget about it and move on.* They're right, in part. The preacher draws on huge reserves of mental energy. Adrenaline surges round the brain and the body before, during, and after preaching. Leaving the pulpit and interacting with those who've heard the sermon puts further demands on the preacher. We stand in a daze as we try to have conversation over a coffee. Our minds are still churning. We're either elated if we feel we've done a good job or deflated if we feel we've mucked it up. Either way, we're coming down from the demands of preaching. Monday is where we finally land, and it's usually not pretty.

Martyn Lloyd-Jones said that he wouldn't cross the street to hear his own preaching. Eric Alexander confessed that his first impulse when out of the pulpit was to say, "Lord, I am sorry."[1] Some of us want to run away from the memory of Sunday's ministry as fast as we can, loudly apologizing for it as we do.

And yet, let's not be too quick to put our post-sermon crash completely down to the flatlining of adrenaline and mental exhaustion. Maybe our moody Mondays tell us more than just how exhausting preaching can be. Could our moods and low spirit be the reminders of what we need to remember most, that we are always weak and sinful people in constant need of a Savior? Perhaps we feel so low on Mondays precisely because we *are* low. Mondays have lessons of grace to teach us.

We need the Monday gospel. Left to ourselves, we are all without hope. Sin and misery are the cycles of our lives. Sin and misery would be the course of our lives as preachers, too. We live in a broken world, and though we often try to deny it, we are broken people. Our commission to preach is a call to see that brokenness up close, in our lives and in the lives of our hearers.

But the gospel sings out the message of hope to us. There is a Redeemer. Christ has come for God's chosen ones in the fullness of saving grace. He lives, he saves, and he loves his people. For us he endured the thistles and thorns of a sin-torn world. All of our

---

1. Cited in Derek J. Prime and Alistair Begg, *On Being a Pastor: Understanding Our Calling and Work* (Chicago: Moody Publishers, 2004), 141.

foolish efforts at being independent of God were heaped upon his head at the cross. He was broken for us. Even for preachers. He has all the grace we need.

Preachers need to pause here and do a little reflecting. Listen to your Monday moods. Don't be too quick to write off post-sermon lowness as just mental and physical exhaustion. Exhausted you probably are; but you are also a sinner. Did your preaching remind you that despite your best cover-up attempts, you're simply a sinner in need of grace? If so, that is a great discovery. The truth is that the congregation knew it all along. And they still love you. Now that you've remembered it, marvel at their love, and marvel at the love of God in Jesus Christ all the more. He came, labored, died, rose, ascended, and is interceding for preachers like you.

13

Knowing Jesus

Q. Does Jesus love preachers?
A. Jesus loves us, and we see that love in his person and offices.

———

He himself likewise partook of the same things, that through death he might destroy the one who has the power of death, that is, the devil.

Hebrews 2:14

Jesus Christ loves preachers. He died for every one of our sins, loves every one of us, delights in any service done in his name, and gives us all the grace we need to minister his Word. Our first calling is not to preach him but to love him and to walk with him. In the words of Samuel Rutherford, "Look up to Him and love Him! O love, and live."[1]

Look to Jesus and love him. There are seasons in your life as a preacher when you can testify to knowing and enjoying Jesus

---

1. Samuel Rutherford, *The Loveliness of Christ* (Edinburgh: Banner of Truth, 2009), 47.

Christ as you prepare sermons and preach them. Preparation times can be rich with a profound sense of fellowship with the risen Lord, as we not only study him in his Word but also by the Holy Spirit sense his nearness. And then there are times when, as you preach Christ, you're overwhelmed by his beauty and his love.

It is such a clear calling but also such a hard one to pursue with hearts like ours in a world like this. Every preacher sets out sincerely believing that he will grow closer to Christ through his preaching. Then he has one of those weeks. Or years. Or decades. A crisis in the family, pain in marriage, conflicts with children, or the trials of singleness; the slow-burn of criticism, or tension with other leaders or church members; the dragging weight of temptation; an overwhelming and at times crushing sense of failure in his ministry. Of course there are many, many encouragements and signs of grace along the way, but struggle is the familiar landscape of many a preacher's life. Oh yes, the Lord is more than able to use all these pressures and many more to bring us close to himself; but for many preachers, these trials, tiring and often protracted difficulties, end up making us spiritually dry and weak in confidence and motivation.

The Lord knows. And the Lord cares about us. Wretched we came to him for our justification, and weak we continue with him as his disciples. No brilliant preaching justifies us, but neither can any terrible preaching damn us. Our strength? It is Jesus, and only him. Not our faith, our gifts, our track record as servants of the gospel, or anything else. So if we want to find our strength again, we need to go back to Jesus, look to him, and live.

And what a magnificent Lord he is. The Westminster Shorter Catechism frames three questions and answers around Christ's full deity and humanity, his incarnation, and his work as Prophet, Priest, and King (Qq. 21–23). Their truth is profound and a feast prepared for our reflection and worship:

Q. 21. Who is the Redeemer of God's elect?

A. The only Redeemer of God's elect is the Lord Jesus Christ, who, being the eternal Son of God, became man, and so was and continues to be God and man, in two distinct natures and one person, forever.

Q. 22. How did Christ, being the Son of God, become man?

A. Christ, the Son of God, became man by taking to himself a true body and a reasonable soul, being conceived by the power of the Holy Ghost in the womb of the Virgin Mary, and being born of her, yet without sin.

Q. 23. What offices does Christ execute as our Redeemer?

A. Christ as our Redeemer executes the offices of a prophet, of a priest, and of a king, both in his estate of humiliation and exaltation.[2]

How wonderful that Jesus is our Prophet, Priest, and King. If you want to anchor these statements in a single passage of Scripture, go to Hebrews 2:12–17. Christ our Prophet declares the will of God to us. He is no angel but the God-man in our flesh, sharing our humanity. He always honored God with the truth, even when it meant the cost of his own life. He speaks the truth to us today, through his Word, in the power of his Holy Spirit. He is our Priest, who lived sinlessly before God and offered our sacrifice for sin in his body at the cross. And he is our King, who has defeated death and has broken the power it once held over all who come to trust in him. This King rules over our lives and calls us to do what is right in God's sight. He gives us generously of his Holy Spirit so that, even in dark days, we can do just that.

Every preacher knows the power of death. Hebrews 2:15 speaks about Jesus's victory to deliver "all those who through fear of death were subject to lifelong slavery." Feel familiar? You see the fear of death overshadowing the lives of those you preach to. You might know it in your own life. What other "deaths" scare you? Hard work? Failure? Criticism? Preachers are a fearful

---

2. *The Westminster Shorter Catechism* (Edinburgh: Banner of Truth, 2015), 12–13.

bunch. With a daily walk with Jesus those fears don't vanish, but they are brought under his control.

Should you know these truths? Absolutely. More than just know them, you must allow them to shape your soul. The old saying (attributed to Thomas Aquinas) affirms, "All true theology teaches us God, is taught by God, and leads us to God." Take that truth, and then remember that as the Word of God, Jesus Christ reveals all truth and brings us to himself and to his Father through it.

So, put Christ before you. Study him and speak to him. Give him your heart. As Peter Martyr Vermigli says: "By divine goodness we have been gathered into the happy army and under the banner of so noble a prince and so great a brother. He will spare neither goodwill nor great power to help us. Let us yield ourselves completely to him."[3]

In 1650 an English businessman was returning from a trip to Scotland. He told a friend that he had heard three preachers there. One showed him the majesty of God, another "showed me all my heart," and then "I heard a little fair man, and he showed me the loveliness of Christ."[4] That little fair man was Samuel Rutherford. The business of preaching is to show our hearers who God is and how much we have fallen short of him and need him. Then we show them Christ in his magnificent saving grace. In looking to him, as Rutherford said, we love, and we live.

That is their deepest need and our great commission. But we must know him first.

3. Peter Martyr Vermigli, *The Peter Martyr Reader*, ed. John Patrick Donnelly, Frank A. James III, and Joseph C. McLelland (Kirksville, MO: Truman State University Press, 1999), 14.

4. Alexander Whyte, *Samuel Rutherford and Some of His Correspondents* (Edinburgh: Oliphant Anderson and Ferrier, 1894), 10.

14

For His Name's Sake

Q. Surely we preachers don't have to suffer, do we?
A. We have no choice but every help as we follow the Jesus who chose to suffer.

———

For it has been granted to you that for the sake of Christ you should not only believe in him but also suffer for his sake.

Philippians 1:29

He sat me down in his office. He was a very well-known preacher, famous for being a little remote and severe, but a deeply loving man. I was a nervous twenty-one-year-old. He was pretty unconvinced of my call to preach (at least that's how I interpreted his severity). He had a clipboard on which he wrote as I spoke. I don't know what purpose it served, but it made me feel small. I only remember one thing he said, which was that if I were to become a preacher, then I better get used to some long hours. That was it. *Long hours.*

I left stunned. I wanted to be given advice and encouragement; and if he had warnings for me, I wanted to hear about something far more scary than a bit of hard work. Having grown up around people who worked hard, I was more than ready for that. I knew that the hours weren't going to be the problem. But I did have a hunch back then that there would be proper suffering ahead. A few years later, I would learn that to become a preacher was to enter a company of men who seemed to attract trouble without looking for it.

Preachers are called to love Jesus and to walk with him. This much is obvious. But equally, the preacher finds that this is a far harder calling than he ever imagined. Maybe we thought we were called "not only to believe on him, but also to preach for him." No one mentioned actual suffering.

Preachers will suffer. Let me add quickly, I know everyone suffers. Faith or no faith, the Bible says we'll discover that life isn't fair and people don't get what they deserve. Part of faith is having to deal with a lot of stuff you would rather not deal with.

Yet preachers do seem to have a large share of struggle. As I think about and pray for my many friends who preach, I'm struck by how many battle with terrible suffering. Among them and their families I list the anguish of severe depression, long-term illness (both mental and physical), financial worries, workplace overload. Compare their trials with a selection of my friends who aren't handling God's Word, and it's hard not to wonder, *why does the lightning always seem to strike us?*

I'm not complaining, nor are they. No preacher worthy of his calling is asking for pity. But every preacher who will fulfill his calling needs to know that suffering will come, and that it will probably set up home with him under his roof. "Endure hardship" is the motto of apostolic ministry (see 2 Tim. 2:3; 4:5).

Endure hardship. Not because it is good for you, like a diet or exercise, but because Jesus did, and our calling is to be transformed in the image of his holiness. He became "perfect through suffering" (Heb. 2:10). That means, Jesus became truly qualified to be our Mediator as he experienced in his human nature all our temptations and entered into all our sorrows. Only then could he offer himself at the cross "without blemish to God" (Heb. 9:14). His sufferings are the pattern for all his people.

Mighty God made fragile baby. No rights, no privileges, few comforts, and every imaginable assault of the Evil One. Then hated and rejected, led out to die, and laid out in death. This is Jesus. This is where his love took him.

> He was led by his love for others into the world, to forget himself in the needs of others, to sacrifice self once for all upon the altar of sympathy. Self-sacrifice brought Christ into the world. And self-sacrifice will lead us, his followers, not away from but into the midst of men. Wherever men suffer, there will we be to comfort. Wherever men strive, there will we be to help. Wherever men fail, there will we be to uplift. Wherever men succeed, there will we be to rejoice. The path of self-sacrifice is the path to glory.[1]

We must go where he calls. Forget the call to preach as a ticket to a comfortable life. Forget the buzz of preaching as being the adrenaline hit for an otherwise dull life. Forget preaching as being the affirmation your heart craves. Christ calls us to lay down our rights and dreams. He is calling us to something altogether bigger, to give ourselves up in his service, which is the service of others.

In that service, the long hours are the easy bit. The preacher's life gets hard when he must face indifference, rejection, exhaustion of spirit and body, and disappointment in his apparent lack of gifts, and all of this year on year. The man with the clipboard didn't warn me that someone would have a stroke in one of my first sermons, or that I would be heckled, or that one particular person would fall asleep every week (and often snore), or that a certain family would pick my sermon apart straight afterward, sometimes loudly enough for me to hear. Why should he tell me

---

1. B. B. Warfield, "Imitating the Incarnation," in *The Savior of the World* (Edinburgh: Banner of Truth, 1991), 270.

the full range of sorrows to come? Why, for that matter, need he tell me of the joys? Along with every other preacher, I would just have to experience the hilarious and the heartbreaking. And all of them would be used by the Holy Spirit to deepen my conviction that God has ordained preaching as his special means of building up the church.

A little suffering along the way? A few tears, some sleepless nights, and various setbacks? Bring it on, if Jesus Christ is glorified and his people are led safely home.

15

Rewarded

Q. Where does our reward come from?
A. Our reward comes from the exalted Christ, and is Christ.

———

Your eyes will behold the king in his beauty;
  they will see a land that stretches afar.
Isaiah 33:17

Suffering is often a powerful test of who we really are. Suffering exposes our values, our faith, and our hearts.

Yet, another test is arguably more effective for exposing who we really are, and that is success. It's as we experience success that we discover why we're really preaching. Success tests us to see if we are proud or if we really are humble, thankful, and trusting.

We see how success brings this exposure again and again in the world and in the Bible. In the world, we've lost count of honorable politicians who've worked so hard to enter public office but then fallen once they've achieved the position they've made sacrifices to win. In the Bible, it's when the people of Israel enter the Promised Land and have initial successes in their conquest that they soon give in to complacency and false religion. It's when Gideon, David, and Solomon taste success that they collapse into catastrophic sin.

Success has many casualties. It can bring out pride and selfishness. Success rarely brings us to our knees, at least not until we're broken by it. Jesus never trusted success in his earthly life and never sought it according to the world's standards. His success was his faith and his humble service to God in order to redeem lost people.

We Christians are convinced that Jesus's pattern of life, heaven included, will be ours. If we are united to him by his Spirit, all that he undergoes—suffering, serving, dying, and then being raised and rewarded—becomes the pattern of our lives. Death will not be our end, any more than it was for Christ. One day, we shall be with him, and we shall be like him (see 1 John 3:2).

We need to think about heaven, and we need to talk about heaven. The gospel makes no sense and has no power unless judgment is real and heaven's reward is eternal. If we preachers deny our hearers this perspective on their trials and tears, then we are failing them. If we lose this perspective on our ministry, whether it's going great or disappointing us, we will put ourselves in great danger of not finishing the race and of missing the true reward.

Most Christians think very little about heaven, and even less about rewards. Preachers are no different. Maybe we think that when we get older, we'll turn our thoughts to eternity. By that stage, though, most can't muster greater faith after years of neglecting to focus on the life to come. Many find themselves beaten down by feelings of guilt and fear. They just hope, in some general way, that things will be "nice" in heaven.

Nice they won't be. Glorious they certainly will. "For a gracious reward the Lord will cause [believers] to possess such a glory as never entered into the heart of man to conceive."[1]

---

1. Belgic Confession (1561), art. 37, in *The Three Forms of Unity* (Birmingham, AL: Solid Ground Christian Books, 2010), 62–63.

The reward is Jesus.

Back in Isaiah's day, the flame of faith was burning low. People were caught up in their problems, and their problems became their distractions. People didn't want the Lord, and they didn't want his word through his servant. Isaiah knew what it was to face mockery, and hostility in various other forms. In chapter 33 of his book, the nation is in crisis. They've broken the terms of their alliance with the current superpower, Assyria, and are about to face Assyrian wrath. And then, in an unexpected fanfare of hope, God gives prophet and people an amazing promise. Having proclaimed his utter trustworthiness (vv. 5–6), he announces,

> Your eyes will behold the king in his beauty;
>> they will see a land that stretches afar. (v. 17)

A king and a land. When their own land was tiny and embattled, and so many of their kings were such a disappointment, could God really do this? And then you look to your ministry. You are often your biggest disappointment, and you look out on your hearers and inwardly groan at how foolish your preaching seems. Can God really make you the man of God you long to be? And will your efforts ever be rewarded?

Just as God was telling his people through Isaiah, the answer is yes. Yes, God will ensure that you receive your reward.

John Calvin comments on this verse,

> Although at present wicked men have everything in their power, and oppress the true servants of God, so that they scarcely have a spot on which they can plant their foot in safety, yet with firm hope we ought to look for our King, who will at length sit down on his bright and magnificent throne, and will gloriously enrich his people.[2]

Every preacher must work and pray to be successful in his ministry. We need to expose that false piety which makes peace with

---

2. John Calvin, *Commentary on the Book of the Prophet Isaiah*, vol. 3, trans. William Pringle, in *Calvin's Commentaries* (Grand Rapids, MI: Baker, 1993), 32–33.

failure under the guise of "being faithful." Says Richard Baxter, "It is a sign of a false, self-seeking heart, that can be content to be still doing, and yet see no fruit of his labour; so I have observed that God seldom blesses any man's work so much as his whose heart is set upon the success of it."[3] Of course, the Lord of the harvest alone can give the increase; but he has given us the mandate of wielding prayer and the Word in order to see people brought to Christ and built up in him. The preacher wants to travel to heaven with as many as he can who are growing with him in their joy in Jesus. In this world, that is success.

And then we are going to heaven, to the King and his land. We shall see him, we shall be like him. For this we labor and pray.

---

3. Richard Baxter, *The Reformed Pastor* (Edinburgh: Banner of Truth, 1989), 121.

16

This Solid Ground

Q. But are we saved?

A. We must neither deceive ourselves about our salvation nor give in to despair.

———

Because of him you are in Christ Jesus, who became to us wisdom from God, righteousness and sanctification and redemption.

1 Corinthians 1:30

Few preachers remember how it all started, but most of us can trace the same problem in our pastoral experience. Somewhere and somehow we started to trust in our sermons. At some point we started to believe that because we were preachers, we could stand confident in ourselves before God. We had something to offer to him. Justification through proclamation, if you will. We know that it is both foolish and dangerous, but like Aaron's calf, which just "happened" to come out of the fire, we put in the effort of preparing and preaching, did it a few times, and out came this misplaced trust (see Ex. 32:24).

Not that we realize it when ministry is plain sailing and we feel the warm smiles of our hearers. They love the sermons, we love preaching them, and the hours spent in the study are a delight. All is well, life and ministry are good, and the Lord smiles, too.

Then the clouds gather, the clouds of disappointment, tiredness, criticism, doubt—even the clouds of a little self-understanding. This task of preaching has beaten us. We know we're not on the verge of heralding revival. No one thinks we're the greatest thing since George Whitefield. We are, though, on the edge of working something out. Two months or twenty years into our work of preaching, and we realize something, something that is devastating to us: we are trusting in our preaching. We have been trusting in it to feel that we can stand before God and before his people. And, oh, we're so wrong.

We are now looking to our preaching to feel like we're somebody in the sight of God. Even the holy calling of proclaiming God's Word, if we trust in it, becomes a "broken reed of a staff, which will pierce the hand of any man who leans on it" (Isa. 36:6). Preaching rarely bears the weight of our expectations. It certainly never bears the weight of our redemption. That is Jesus's task, and no one and nothing will do that in his place.

Jesus is and always will be the Redeemer. First Corinthians 1:30 is a rich seam of saving truth: "Because of him you are in Christ Jesus, who became to us wisdom from God, righteousness and sanctification and redemption." We preachers can never get enough of this truth. It must master us, subduing our pride in success, and lifting and comforting us in disaster.

This part of 1 Corinthians 1 is Paul's challenge to our worldly way of seeking out human power and what appears to be impressive, and the reassertion of God's power and wisdom through the cross of Jesus Christ. The cross looks and is foolish to a dying world, but it is God's power for believers (v. 18). Paul reminds the Corinthians that a world full of apparently wise people only ends up failing to discern God (vv. 20–21). In this supposedly wise but actually foolish world, God has set his own message of the cross. This message will always be controversial, mocked, and opposed. Those who believe it will discover that this "foolishness" and this "weakness" are in fact God's wisdom and power (vv. 22–25).

How much we preachers need to remind ourselves of this. No human wisdom gets us to God; only God's wisdom can bring us to him. This is his achievement in the cross. It is never something we ourselves have worked out or deserve any credit for realizing. In fact, read verses 26–30: when we are tempted toward Corinthian boasting in ourselves, we need to remember that we really aren't anything special but are maybe even some of the weak and foolish whom God has chosen in order to shame the wise and strong (v. 27). Our trouble is that we think far too much of ourselves, and our danger is that we often think far too little of Christ and the wonder of his cross.

Here's a recommendation: if you know you are tempted to look to your preaching for your justification and are troubled by it, take the medicine of verse 30—reflect on who Jesus Christ is and all the riches of God's grace offered to us in him. Pause, meditate, reflect, wonder, praise, confess, and commit. Before him there can be no boasting. And in him there is true life.

Christ is our redemption. Is there no place for our preaching in our salvation? No power in it to save us? None whatsoever. It is all of grace through faith.

Many years ago my wife cut out a quotation from Spurgeon and put it on our fridge. When we felt overwhelmed by ministry, crushed by our failures as spouses and parents, and mine as a preacher, Spurgeon's words were a great help to our souls, and still are:

> Remember, therefore, it is not your hold of Christ that saves you—it is Christ; it is not your joy in Christ that saves you—it is Christ; it is not even faith in Christ, though that be the instrument—it is Christ's blood and merits; therefore, look not so much to your hand with which you are grasping Christ, as

to Christ; look not to your hope, but to Jesus, the source of your hope; look not to your faith, but to Jesus, the author and finisher of your faith. We shall never find happiness by looking at our prayers, our doings, or our feelings; it is what Jesus is, not what we are, that gives rest to the soul.[1]

---

1. C. H. Spurgeon, *Morning and Evening* (Fearn, Ross-shire: Christian Focus, 1998), 378 (entry for June 28).

17

Lavish Love

Q. How can we know we really are saved?
A. Our true identity is found not in being busy preachers but in being called to be sons of God.

———

See what kind of love the Father has given to us, that we should be called children of God.

1 John 3:1

A preacher is usually at the heart of his church family. For full-time pastors, there is a deeply privileged access into people's lives as they open up about their joys and struggles. Who doesn't feel deeply humbled when people open up and share something intensely personal, or feel the great privilege of bringing them the Word of the living God?

And yet, being so immersed in the lives of others can often leave us feeling that we're at the edge of things. I was recently preaching in a church of another tradition, which meant that I had to process in and out of the worship service and sit in an appointed seat. I felt the congregation's respect, but I also felt at a distance from them because of a barrier I needed to overcome. Regardless of our ways of doing things even in our own churches, we preachers all feel at times that we're out on a limb, at the same time belonging yet struggling with a distance from others who aren't sure how to relate to "the Bible man."

Sometimes church itself makes us feel least confident that we belong to the church. I'm not thinking so much of the sins people commit against us (insert here the latest slight you've received after a sermon); I'm thinking more of the ways in which we let the church down with our preaching mistakes and blunders. Once we loved the thought of being set apart as the preacher. Now we are so often disappointed in our preaching, and we fear that others are, too.

Most of us who preach lurch between pride and despair, often in the same day. We puff ourselves up, delighted to be preachers. Says Spurgeon, "The pride of knowing replaces the humility of being known."[1] And then, we fail in our task and are in the depths. The remedy is never that we should seek some stoic resignation in the highs and lows of ministry—never too up, never too down. The remedy is in the gospel, and especially in the gospel truth that in Christ we are adopted into God's family.

The doctrine of adoption is vital for the preacher. We are not preachers first; we are not primarily servants, called to a round of preaching and teaching. Those things are secondary at best. Above everything else, we are sons, the adopted sons of God. We are children, with all of God's people. The Father has lavished his great love upon us to make us the children of God (1 John 3:1). The Son has given us the right to become those children (John 1:12), and declares his delight in us as his brothers (Heb. 2:12–13). "The Spirit himself bears witness with our spirit that we are children of God" (Rom. 8:16). Salvation belongs to the Lord (Jonah 2:9),

---

1. Paul David Tripp, *Dangerous Calling: Confronting the Unique Challenges of Pastoral Ministry* (Nottingham: Inter-Varsity Press, 2012), 196.

and that salvation finds its most beautiful expression in our adoption as his children. As J. I. Packer says, "Justification is the basic blessing, on which adoption is founded; adoption is the crowning blessing, to which justification clears the way."[2]

Forget the grace of your adoption, and your delight in the Lord will be in peril. The difficulties of your calling to preach will weigh you down, and you'll struggle to know where to find help. Your failures will tempt you to see your loving Father as a "hard man" (Matt. 25:24), demanding, grasping, and never satisfied. You will see your preaching as a treadmill, going nowhere and never stopping, an endless assignment set for you by a distant God. Your preaching will lose grace and gentleness, and then everyone will be in trouble.

The remedy is memory. Remember that you're a child of God and you have a heart's feast in the midst of your work. You know that your Father's love is always with you. Sometimes your preaching is atrocious, usually it's all right, and just occasionally it's brilliant. Your Father knows, and his love for you is absolutely constant. Hard work for his sake is the privilege we get to do as an act of worship. It is the natural activity of children who know their Father's smile.

And the people you preach to? If we either see ourselves as "above" them or even feel that our failings as preachers separate us from them, we need to go back to the gospel and learn afresh the work of Christ. Those who are born-again believers are our brothers and sisters. We have been bought by the same blood and share the same family name. We have the one Spirit to drink from together (1 Cor. 12:13). Together with them, we call on the same Father and are loved just as the Father loves the Son (John 17:23). We all rely on the same Father to supply all our needs (Phil. 4:19). And we look forward to the same shared inheritance. Even if we feel that the work sometimes causes a distance between our

---

2. J. I. Packer, *Concise Theology: A Guide to Historic Christian Beliefs* (Leicester: Inter-Varsity Press, 1993), 167.

hearers and us, we must remember that the divide doesn't actually exist. We are all members of the family of grace.

Knowing our adoption contains power. We are set free from the temptation of trying to impress our hearers or our God. "We are unworthy servants; we have only done what was our duty" (Luke 17:10). This is true. Just so, we are blood-bought, adopted children, who have done our delight of loving our Father and our brothers and sisters as we've declared his Word. Knowing that we're in the family of God brings comfort, peace, and identity.

18

Holiness

Q. How will we preachers grow?
A. We must live in God's peace and pursue holiness.

———

Put on the Lord Jesus Christ.
Romans 13:14

To reverse the oft-quoted words of Robert Murray M'Cheyne, an unholy preacher is a useless weapon in the hands of God.

Do preachers grow in holiness by preaching? The Lord Jesus Christ preached a lot, and he was sinless—so, we might reason, won't preparing sermons and preaching help us in the way of holiness? We tell ourselves that enough time spent studying God's Word and some more proclaiming it, and we will grow to be like Jesus Christ. Surely we can preach our way into sanctification, can't we?

God isn't so confident. Obviously, studying the Word and thinking through its meaning are essential for all Christian growth. But the Bible-mandated ways of growing in grace are for preachers as much as anyone else. In the light of God's Word we must identify our sins and repent of them; in their place we must think through new habits of godliness; we must pray specific prayers with discipline; we must put ourselves right into the fellowship of God's people, serving, sharing, and learning; we must learn to live out our baptism, take the Lord's Supper, and sit under good preaching. Merely preaching will not grow us in godliness.

Paul commanded Timothy to watch his life and his doctrine closely (1 Tim. 4:16). Preachers discover (especially when they fail) that those who listen to them, week in and week out, have been watching their preachers' lives all along, often very closely. Hearers are asking the questions—whether they've realized it or not—is this man's life attractive? And is it attractively different from mine? If the answer to these is yes, then those listeners want to find out what their pastor has. They'll listen all the more carefully to what the preacher says.

Preaching is the commitment to showing our hearers from the Word that Jesus is powerfully real. Our growth in grace must not only back up our words; it must also display the real and powerful Jesus in our lives. Why should people want to hear your doctrine if your life is unattractive? Why should they believe that the message is life-transforming if the messenger's life is the same as anyone else's?

Hang on, though; this sounds very much like the preacher's holiness is critical to the success of his ministry. This sounds like I'm saying that if we don't grow in grace, God won't build his kingdom through us. Isn't this putting far too much importance on the preacher himself? What about Balaam's ass, the donkey who spoke God's word? No holiness there, but a harvest of blessing for God's people, and glory to God. And what about Paul's insistence that as long as the gospel is preached, we needn't fret too much about the motives of those doing it (Phil. 1:15–18)? Isn't our job just to lead hearers to Christ in his Word and leave them with him?

No. We preachers can't evade the plain truth that God uses holy men for his holy work. Paul urges Timothy to pursue holiness in order to be useful to the Lord's purposes (2 Tim. 2:21). The apostle again reasons that without personal holiness, God's servant not only jeopardizes his own profession of faith but also undermines the salvation of others (1 Tim. 4:15–16). It is that serious.

We must be holy. If we neglect this calling, we may well end up preaching ourselves, or getting in the way of our Master. If so, our unholiness will actually obscure the glory of Christ. If we are dull, if we are unmoved by the truths we handle in the pulpit, if an illustration we use is self-promoting or inappropriate for some other reason, if our words aren't conveying love and tenderness (the list could go on), then we are getting in the way of the beauty of Jesus. People can't see Christ and won't hear the gospel for the truth it is, because our lives aren't actually displaying Christ.

John the Baptist was a burning and a shining light (John 5:35). He didn't always make for comfortable listening for the crowds, but the crowds came to see him and to hear him. The Lord might not give us crowds, but as M'Cheyne himself prayed, our longing should be to be as holy as a pardoned sinner can be. Only as we grow to be like Jesus are we effective in showing him to others in our lives and through our proclamation.

Does this sound intimidating? Actually, it's the opposite. The call is to taste life in Jesus, the only life that satisfies and is worth living. Grace is at work in our holiness: therefore, we *can* grow and we *will* grow. As Jared Wilson says, "Holiness is Christlikeness, and we who are justified by Christ will be sanctified in Christ and glorified with Christ."[1] Christ is being formed in us by his Holy Spirit. We have an ocean of God's love to experience, knowing assurance of our forgiveness, resting in the peace of God, tasting more and more joy in the Spirit, and being so confident that the grace we're tasting is the very same grace that will see us all

---

1. Jared C. Wilson, *The Pastor's Justification: Applying the Work of Christ in Your Life and Ministry* (Wheaton, IL: Crossway, 2013), 57.

the way to glory. Who wouldn't want to know more and more of this gospel love, and who wouldn't want to live it out?

So, preacher, grow in grace. Allow the Word you handle so often for others to speak into your life. Allow it to pierce you and open you up, as well as to heal and comfort you. Listen to its instruction. Pray gospel truth through, and pray it in. Then live it out in a life of deepening holiness. Take specific steps to beat specific sins. Put on holiness. Clothe yourself with Jesus Christ (Rom. 13:14). And let your communion with Christ express itself in your ministry.

Do it. For Jesus's sake—and for theirs.

19

Journey's End

Q. Will we ever stop preaching?
A. Our preaching will die, and so will we. That is good news!

––––––

There is laid up for me the crown of righteousness, which the
Lord, the righteous judge, will award to me on that day, and
not only to me but also to all who have loved his appearing.

2 Timothy 4:8

Every preacher knows that the hardest part is knowing when to
finish. As you prepare, when do you know that you've covered all
that you need to (and not too much)? And in the pulpit, how do
you make that decision that people have got it and that you must
now finish? Like a pilot in a plane, landing the thing can be the
hardest part.

And then compare that to knowing when to finish your ministry. You may preach for many years, and your preaching may
be much appreciated; or may have been. You have been called,

and you have been obedient to the Lord. When do you know that you've completed your task and now must lay it down? In all the books I have about ministry and preaching, not one addresses this topic. A fuller answer is beyond the scope of this chapter, and anyway, I don't have an answer. I do have some observations and some questions. Above all, I want to raise the issue and to show how the Westminster Shorter Catechism reflects the gospel, and so helps us think about it.

Some preachers go on and on, with God's blessing and people's appreciation. The Puritan Thomas Goodwin was preaching powerfully right up to a few days before his death, aged almost eighty. John Wesley preached all the way to his death at eighty-seven. There are preachers in their nineties whose ministries are still valued. The wisdom of many decades has been distilled with great effect in the ministries of older men and is much appreciated.

The opposite is also true. Some men can't stop, even when they should. A stubborn determination to keep on keeping on grips them, even when it is obvious to all that the blessing isn't there anymore in their ministry. They see a glory in long ministries, and who doesn't? But the only lasting glory is in a ministry that serves God by building up his people. Once a preacher is no longer able to do that, even if he can still get in the pulpit and wants to, it is time to stop.

Warning his students of the need to keep a servant-hearted attitude as full-time preachers, Charles Spurgeon said, "Ministers are for churches, and not churches for ministers. In our work among the churches, we must not dare to view them as estates to be farmed for our own profit, or gardens to be trimmed to our own taste."[1]

That is our temptation, isn't it? Whether we serve as pastors or as regular or even occasional preachers, we are tempted to look on the church as something that exists for our gratification. We love to prepare, and we love to preach. Of course, this enjoyment is a

1. C. H. Spurgeon, *An All-Round Ministry* (Edinburgh: Banner of Truth, 1965), 256.

gift from God to be received with thanksgiving. But if our enjoyment begins and ends with these things and not the good of the flock, then everyone's in trouble.

Of course, the man who stops preaching *feels* the loss of it. Of course, he *feels* incomplete. But he must remind himself that he *isn't*. His call was to serve the church in a particular way. He has done that, and now he must put it aside. Naked he came to preaching, and naked he left it. Blessed be the name of the Lord.

The Westminster Shorter Catechism is helpful here:

Q. 37. What benefits do believers receive from Christ at death?

A. The souls of believers are at their death made perfect in holiness, and immediately pass into glory; and their bodies, being still united to Christ, rest in their graves, till the resurrection.[2]

Preachers die. And preachers live again, like every Christian. We have a glorious guaranteed future ahead of us because of Christ. This is the preacher-saving gospel.

Q. 38. What benefits do believers receive from Christ at the resurrection?

A. At the resurrection, believers, being raised up in glory, shall be openly acknowledged and acquitted in the day of judgment, and made perfectly blessed in the full enjoying of God to all eternity.[3]

"Acquitted in the day of judgment." We'll be acquitted of all of our sins through Christ, and of all of our preaching and ministry sins, too. Even if we have sixty years of preaching behind us and have led thousands to a closer walk with Christ, it will be Christ alone who acquits us. We will never earn our salvation.

The thought of our appearing before Christ gives us encouragement as well as reason for honesty about our preaching and our preaching motivations. Here are five questions:

---

2. *The Westminster Shorter Catechism* (Edinburgh: Banner of Truth, 2015), 19.
3. *Shorter Catechism*, 20.

1. Do I preach because I need to or because others need my ministry?
2. Does the thought of laying down my preaching ministry in old age fill me with dread or quicken my thoughts about heaven?
3. Will I be content one day to be thought of as an "ex-preacher," or do I hanker after the affirmation I believe that preaching brings me?
4. Do I privately long that people will remember all my sermons, or is the knowledge that God's Word has fed them (whether they remember my sermons or not, and even forget me) enough for me?
5. What do the words "well done, good and faithful servant" really say to my soul?

One day, Mr. Preacher, you will have preached yourself to silence. Your work will be done, and your reward will be ready. Christ will be the end of all your preaching, quite literally. Live with that day in sight, and look forward to it.

Part 3

———

Loving
the Word

20

The Grace of Law

Q. Must we preachers obey the law, too?
A. The law is the guide to our holiness, and an unholy preacher
is a fraud.

———

Set the believers an example in speech, in conduct, in love, in
faith, in purity.

1 Timothy 4:12

Preachers of Jesus must be like Jesus. No one will listen to a man
to learn Christ if they cannot look at him and see Christ.

One of our great temptations as preachers is to feel that our
ministry is enough for God. Ministry is the sacrifice we give to
him. Surely God is satisfied when we give ourselves sacrificially
to preparing our sermons and then deliver them just as well as we
can, isn't he? Surely he is glorified as his Word is preached, right?
So can't we rest satisfied that if we persevere in preaching ministry,
we can look forward to our "well done, good and faithful servant"?

Giving God service, even sweat-induced, exhaustion-bringing service, is the soft option. God wants more, but he may not be after more of our service. God wants our hearts, not only our hands. He wants to capture our wills, to bring us to his heart, so that we know that "deep speaks to deep." God wants us to love him and to express that love in holy living. The rest—including our preaching—is detail.

"Set the believers an example in speech, in conduct, in love, in faith, in purity" was Paul's counsel (1 Tim. 4:12). He was writing to Timothy in the latter's tough job of preaching Christ in the metropolis of Ephesus. Feeling keenly his inexperience and probably daunted by Ephesus's godless trinity of sex, money, and paganism, Timothy was urged to stand firm. More than that, he was commanded to press on, and to press on in godliness. Whatever he did as preacher and pastor, Timothy needed to grow in grace. In this city where everyone was out to get what he could, Timothy was to grow to be more like the Lord Jesus Christ. That is not optional, not for this young preacher, nor for us.

The law reveals who God is and what he is like. It also shows us who we are and what we are like. God is the Lord, he is holy, and he demands worship. We, on the other hand, are not lords of our lives but have been created to be dependent on God, and to honor him as we obey his law. We also discover, though, that we are unholy people: we do not naturally want to obey him, nor can we even do so.

The poet Christina Rossetti captures well the reality of indwelling sin in the believer. She begins her poem "Who Shall Deliver Me?"[1] (an obvious reference to the apostle Paul's question in Rom. 7:24) with this verse:

God strengthen me to bear myself;
That heaviest weight of all to bear,
Inalienable weight of care.

1. Christina G. Rossetti, "Who Shall Deliver Me?," in *The Complete Poems of Christina Rossetti*, ed. R. W. Crump, vol. 1 (Baton Rouge, LA: Louisiana State University Press, 1990), 226.

She continues with her confession, startling to unbelievers, but one the Christian recognizes and shares:

> Myself, arch-traitor to myself;
> My hollowest friend, my deadliest foe,
> My clog whatever road I go.

Her conclusion is the gospel answer, sweet to all who receive it:

> Yet One there is can curb myself,
> Can roll the strangling load from me,
> Break off the yoke and set me free.

Jesus breaks the yoke and delivers us into gospel freedom. What we learn is that we're not free to do whatever we feel like (experience shows that there is no freedom in self-will), but we're free to obey God's will. Jesus says that discipleship means bearing his yoke (Matt. 11:28), a yoke which he makes sure is easy for us.

"Do not think that I have come to abolish the Law or the Prophets; I have not come to abolish them but to fulfill them" (Matt. 5:17). What does this important verse mean? It means that Jesus's manifesto was one of jaw obedience. What he pledged to do, he delivered on. He always obeyed the law and fulfilled the meaning of the prophets' writings. Jesus may have been a human tradition breaker and opinion offender, but he was never a law-breaker. And as the One who fulfilled the law, he kept the sacrificial law for us: that means, not only did the law keeper obey where we lawbreakers have failed, but he also became a sacrifice for us according to God's law when he died at the cross.

The implications for us are overwhelming. We are free from the curse of the law if our trust is in Jesus (Gal. 3:13). We have been given life by his Spirit to know him as our Savior and Lord. The same Spirit puts power into our renewed hearts, not only to want to know and obey God's law but increasingly to keep it, to God's glory.

Victories are hard-won, of course, and setbacks are frequent; but more and more we learn the wisdom of God's law for us, and we experience the joy and the freedom there is for us as we pray into our lives its truth and start to bear the fruit of obedience. We grow in love, joy, peace, patience, kindness, and the many other defining characteristics of the "law man" Jesus Christ. We run in the path of his commands with liberated hearts (Ps. 119:32), and it is very, very good.

21

Obedience

Q. What ten things must every preacher know and do?
A. We must know God's law and know why we both preach
it and seek to obey it.

———

I will run in the way of your commandments
    when you enlarge my heart!
Psalm 119:32

People in churches don't really like to talk much about God's
law, and most preachers follow the same inclination. The reasons for this are many. A God who likes law doesn't sound
very fun, some reason. Others point out that his law in the Old
Testament has some strange and clearly outdated parts to it
(sacrificing animals, a ban on eating shrimp, a ban on wearing
mixed fibers, that sort of thing). Besides, isn't the New Testament negative about the law in many passages? Aren't we saved

from it? People disagree over the law, so why bring up something so contentious when we have so much else to agree on? And anyway, didn't Jesus come to abolish the law and to give us the Spirit in its place?

The preacher's calling involves understanding the place of the law of God in the life of God's people. We must understand why God gave the law to his people Israel, and then what place the law has in the life of the Christian today. Only when we're clear about these things can we help our hearers. No one said that this would be easy. Handling the law correctly as Christians is "the greatest knot in the practical part of divinity," said Samuel Bolton.[1] If we are to help the people of God grow in Christ, though, we have no choice. As John Newton wrote, "Ignorance of the nature and design of the law is at the bottom of most religious mistakes."[2]

What so many Christians overlook is the simple but far-reaching truth that the law comes from God. That is the lesson of the theophany at Sinai, as God shows and then declares himself to be the Lord of his people (Ex. 19:16–20:2). The Westminster Shorter Catechism puts it like this:

> Q. 44. What does the preface to the Ten Commandments teach us?
>
> A. The preface to the Ten Commandments teaches us that because God is the Lord, and our God, and Redeemer, therefore we are bound to keep all of his commandments.[3]

Our question, then, is what does it look like for Christians to be "bound" to keep the law? Listen to the counsel of Newton's close friend William Cowper. In a poem-turned-hymn titled "Love Constrained to Obedience," Cowper gives us rich and sound theology that nourishes the life of discipleship:

---

1. Bolton (1606–1654) was a Puritan pastor and scholar. This quotation comes from his *The True Bounds of Christian Freedom* (Edinburgh: Banner of Truth, 1964), 51.

2. John Newton, "On the Right Use of the Law," letter 30 in *The Works of John Newton*, 6 vols. (Edinburgh: Banner of Truth, 1985), 1:340.

3. *The Westminster Shorter Catechism* (Edinburgh: Banner of Truth, 2015), 21–22.

To see the Law by Christ fulfilled,
To hear his pardoning voice,
Changes a slave into a child,
And duty into choice.[4]

Cowper is right. Christ alone keeps the law for us in his obedience for our sakes, and he alone dies for us under the penal sentence of God for our lawbreaking. Slaves are redeemed and adopted into God's family, and a new nature is given to us. And the law? As Cowper shows us, our law keeping as believers is turned from resentful and failing duty into choice. Choice? Yes, it's a Spirit-empowered life of joyful obedience to God through Christ. Therefore, as Kevin DeYoung says, "The law can, and should, be urged upon true believers—not to condemn them, but to correct and to promote Christlikeness."[5] And let's begin with ourselves.

Jesus now teaches us by his Spirit to obey his Word. Does that include the Ten Commandments? Yes, of course. They are the essence of the law of our Redeemer-King. The commands are given by him and bring us to him, and they are the way we enjoy daily fellowship with him. "For this is the love of God, that we keep his commandments. And his commandments are not burdensome" (1 John 5:3). By obeying his law, we remain in Jesus's love (John 15:10).

As we study the Ten Commandments in order to obey them, we must remember that they're all about Jesus. Each shows our need of him and teaches us how to follow him. In the Sermon on the Mount, Jesus restated the commandments and set out both

---

4. William Cowper, *The Poetical Works of William Cowper*, vol. 2 (Edinburgh: James Nichol, 1854), 54. Ralph Erskine teaches the same in this memorable excerpt:

A rigid master was the law,
Demanding brick, denying straw;
But when with gospel-tongue it sings,
It bids me fly, and gives me wings.

The Sermons and Practical Works of Ralph Erksine, vol. 10 (Glasgow: Smith and Bryce, 1778), 283.

5. Kevin DeYoung, *The Hole in Our Holiness: Filling the Gap between Gospel Passion and the Pursuit of Godliness* (Wheaton, IL: Crossway, 2012), 56.

the demands and the promises of a life of discipleship. But he did that only because he had already given those commandments at another mountain, Sinai. He is the giver and center of those and all of God's commands.

This is a vital truth to teach in the pulpit. So often God's people think that the Commandments are a precursor to Jesus. True, they serve as a mirror to show us our unholiness, so that we know that we need the grace of Christ; but we must learn to read and obey them as the commands Jesus has given, which enable us to express our love for him as we keep them.

In our house my wife painted part of a wall with chalk paint. We can doodle, leave notes, put up shopping lists, and write up memory verses. A few weeks ago I wrote—or perhaps rewrote—the Ten Commandments. Heretical? You decide. The Ten Commandments as we've been discussing them round our dinner table read like this:

1. Put nothing in the place of Jesus.
2. Make nothing which gets in the way of your love for Jesus.
3. Honour Jesus' Name in all you do.
4. Seek your soul's rest in Jesus.
5. Honour your parents, as a love-expression for Jesus.
6. Do not murder, as Jesus brings life, never death.
7. Keep sexually pure, because Jesus has won your body, as well as your heart.
8. Do not steal, because Jesus is enough.
9. Do not lie, because Jesus is the truth, and loves the truth.
10. Don't set your heart on anything, because Jesus really is enough.

Maybe you find this way of putting it helpful. The priority is that you see that Jesus is the Lord of the law. Find your own way of having that truth sink in to your soul. And then ask yourself, what sort of cowardice or cruelty would stop us from declaring God's Jesus-law from our pulpits? Why would we not want to preach the Ten Commandments to those seeking Christ, as well as to those who are in Christ? Here we see the One of whom all the Scriptures speak. Here we listen to his voice. Here we see the beauty of his holiness. And here we receive his command to go and live this life. Let's seek grace to do that.

22

Love's Choice

Q. What does the first commandment teach us?
A. You shall preach as a love expression to the Lord your God.

———

I am the LORD your God, who brought you out of the land
of Egypt, out of the house of slavery. You shall have no other
gods before me.

Exodus 20:2–3

A friend of mine has a difficult marriage. He and his wife are
both committed Christians, bravely navigating the stormy waters
of their marriage, but twenty years on it's very tough. Before his
wedding I wrote to him with this piece of advice I came across:
"Choose your love, and love your choice." I've reminded him of
those words over the years, especially when it's been really hard.

Choose your love; God did. Sinai thunders out the truth that
God has chosen and gathered a people to himself. He has already
shown them his love, redeeming his people from Egypt with a

mighty hand and outstretched arm (Ps. 136:12). Now they assemble at his command to hear his word.

At Mount Sinai, God is essentially declaring to his people, "I have chosen you, to love you, and I will love you. And as I have chosen you, choose me and love me. And you will know life as you love me" (cf. Deut. 30:20).

The first commandment is a call to know God—not in some vague, fuzzy way, but to know God as he is, the living God of pursuing, relentless love. This is the God who reveals himself in Jesus Christ (John 1:18; 14:6) and calls us to belong to him through Christ and to discover the saving love he has for lost people. "You shall have no other gods before me" may sound harsh, aggressive, and even threatening to secular ears. Addicted to choice and to doing what feels right to us, our age hears this command and recoils. Like Pharaoh in Egypt, our society angrily says that it doesn't know him and certainly has no intention of doing what he says (cf. Ex. 5:2).

To his redeemed people, by contrast, this is a call to freedom, to throw out the life-stealing false values and loves of our hearts, and to choose and know the God who has chosen us.

"I am the LORD your God, who brought you out of the land of Egypt, out of the house of slavery" (Ex. 20:2). God declares his rescuing and covenant name. As rescuer and covenant maker, he is also owner of his people. As rescuer and owner, he has sovereign rights over us, to call us to loving obedience. The commandment says, "This is your God"; but only obedience says, "This is *my* God."

The commandment is a call to life, to live the whole of our lives as a response of worship to God, loving him, honoring him in every single thing we do.

Preachers, though, feel the pull to want anything but God. Job satisfaction, influence, intellectual stimulation, personal gratification, a quiet life (or a noisy, hectic life), peer group approval, or congregational applause—what's on your wish list? Often we're just not aware of our darkest desires, or we've dressed them up to make them sound very worthy, even when we're only trying to fool ourselves into thinking that all is well. We tell ourselves that we're seeking this or that "blessing" from God. The truth is, we're seeking a certain lifestyle or reward. Whether or not God is in it is of little concern to us.

The first commandment exposes our religious game playing. "Choose me," God demands of us. And yes, sovereign power can lay a command on our affections, all the more so if he's the God of perfect, life-bringing love. Choose the Lord when life is hard, when ministry is unproductive, when it all seems like a frustrating time, when all the scenery of life is the same dreary desert, and when the Promised Land is a very long way off. Choose the Lord.

We preachers often content ourselves (and yes, try to justify ourselves) in the fact that we are quite good at getting rid of the grosser sins from our lives. We've fought our battles and won some victories. Our lives are, generally speaking, fairly consistent, and our ministries are often appreciated. And yet our lives can be so very far from actually keeping this commandment to love God and honor him alone.

The Heidelberg Catechism (1563) treats the commandment in this unforgettable way:

> Q. 94. What does the Lord require in the first commandment?
>
> A. That I, not wanting to endanger my very salvation, avoid and shun all idolatry, magic, superstitious rites, and prayer to saints or to other creatures. That I sincerely acknowledge the only true God, trust him alone, look to him for every good thing humbly and patiently, love him, fear him, and honour him with all my heart. In short, that I give up anything rather than go against his will in any way.[1]

As you reread the answer, note that the first sentence is standard Reformation fare, warning you away from a fascination with both the Roman Catholic Mass and things that go bump in the night.

---

1. *Our Faith: Ecumenical Creeds, Reformed Confessions, and Other Resources* (Grand Rapids: MI: Faith Alive Christian Resources, 2013), 104.

The second sentence floods your heart with both challenging and exalting truth: will you really believe that your God can and will meet all your needs, so that you will bring him all of the love and trust he is so very worthy of? He wants all of your heart, preacher, and unless he has that, he is satisfied by none of your ministry.

God is not reserved, cold, aloof. He is not standoffish. Through his Son, God stands among us, comes to us, embraces us, reassures us, encourages us. He is the God who touched Mount Sinai and made it shake; he's also the God-man who died on Mount Calvary. He loves us, and he wants us to know that he loves us. Even when we can't feel his presence, the gospel teaches us that he is always with us, and that his arms are always round us.

You have to know this. Because if you don't know this, this command will always sound like a demand only, and you will always feel ambivalent about it. More than that, it'll stay on its stone tablet. If you are not convinced that God is kind and tenderhearted, and are not experiencing this love, it'll meet a stony heart—yours. Obedience will feel like dragging a stone around. Unless . . .

Unless you know who it is who's talking to you. Unless you know that your God is your Redeemer, your husband, your Good Shepherd, your friend, the one who has died for you and come back from the grave, who reigns on high, ruling in love and wisdom over your life, and preparing a place for you so that you might dwell with him forever. If you know that this God loves you, delights in you, died to save you, and sent his Spirit to empower you to love him, the obedience becomes what it really is, a blood-bought and Spirit-enabled privilege.

That is the call of the Ten Commandments. And that is the call of this commandment. It is the call of God that we know God, and love him as we know him. God doesn't want to give you knowledge about himself for its own sake. He doesn't give you commands only because he is Lord. He gives you knowledge and commands so that you will bring to him the response of your heart and delight to love him with all your heart, soul, mind, and strength. Choose him.

23

Image Rights?

Q. What does the second commandment teach us?
A. You shall not make a preaching idol of your image or of anyone else's.

————

You shall not make for yourself a carved image, or any likeness of anything that is in heaven above, or that is in the earth beneath, or that is in the water under the earth. You shall not bow down to them or serve them, for I the LORD your God am a jealous God.

Exodus 20:4–5

In the second commandment, God is telling us: "Don't trust anyone or anything to give you the life only I can give you. Trust me. Come to me for life." Hearing the commandment like this changes our suspicion that God is grasping after our affirmation, like a needy and insecure boss or the family's new puppy. God doesn't need us. Quite the opposite, we need him, and the commandment calls us to discover that he is all we need and all we can and should find lasting delight in.

Adam and Eve found something they thought was better than God. They were charged with the highest privilege of knowing the God of glory. They swapped that commission for a mouthful of fruit and the lie that true life can be found away from God.

We are no different. We all operate on a pleasure principle. We are all built to seek happiness (even if the happiness of some consists in being unhappy and maybe trying to make others share in that unhappiness). We all decide what we want in life to make life pleasurable, and we go about getting it and then hanging onto it. Just like Adam and Eve, we mistrust the One who offers life, and we seek it anywhere but in him.

Stephen Charnock (1628–1680) described it like this:

> [Each person] acts so as if . . . God could not make him happy without the addition of something else. Thus the glutton makes a god of his dainties; the ambitious man of his honor; the [lustful] man of his lust; and the covetous man of his wealth; and consequently esteems them as his chiefest good, and the most noble end, to which he directs his thoughts.[1]

It's true. We take the God-given impulse to love and find delight in him, and we turn that impulse onto his world. God has richly given us all things to enjoy (1 Tim. 6:17), but in our sin we enjoy them and reject our Creator. And that is idolatry.

This is why the second commandment is such wonderful good news. God is identifying that default setting we have since the fall, to turn to anything but him to find our deepest longings met. He is urging us to not enslave our hearts, and calling us to be free, free to rest in his love.

John Donne (1572–1631) understood this. Donne chased life's treasures in wild living, political power, the pursuit of money, and then the contentment of marriage and children. He also knew

---

1. Stephen Charnock, *Discourses upon the Existence and Attributes of God* (New York: Robert Carter, 1874), 148.

life's bitterness, losing siblings in childhood and later in adult life, struggling for financial security, and then facing the heaviest blow, the loss of his wife. Through joy and sorrow, he eventually came to find peace in the love of Jesus Christ, and through his poetry and preaching (he later served as dean of St. Paul's Cathedral) he set forth the captivating love of Christ. Above all, he needed God's love in Christ to be jealous: "Oh, if Thou carest not whom I love, Alas! Thou lovest not me."[2]

Do you see Donne's discovery? God *cares* for his people with a perfect love. That is what his jealousy is. God could not conceive of loving lost people and being indifferent as they go their own way, the way of death. He loves. He warns! The opposite of love is not hatred; it's indifference—"I don't care." But love does care. God will have us for himself. And that is the call, and the power, of the gospel.

We preachers need to understand the command as much as anyone else, not only that we can preach its message to others but also that we can first apply it to our discipleship as preachers. We of all people face the most subtle but dangerous temptations to idolatry.

The new preacher finds that he has entered an intoxicating new world, now that he has begun to preach. He speaks and people listen. If he felt invisible in church before, he's got everyone's attention now. More than that, he begins to grow in understanding the Scriptures, as preparation means that he's poring over the Bible text and consulting commentaries. Friends notice growth in gifting and understanding, and make admiring comments. He's thrilled to be serving people in this new, powerful way. He feels closer to God. Prayer has taken on a new urgency, and answered prayer gives him a deep thrill. And he starts to talk to other preachers, who affirm him and underline what he's starting to feel about the importance (and difficulty) of preaching.

---

2. John Donne, "A Hymne to Christ, at the Author's Last Going into Germany" (1617), in *Metaphysical Lyrics and Poems of the Seventeenth Century*, ed. Herbert J. C. Grierson (Oxford: Oxford University Press, 1962), 90.

This all good, but it's not without its dangers. Delight in preaching can rival devotion to the Lord. The Bible can be a book we teach to others rather than apply to our own souls. Preaching can be something we love to do for its apparent rewards, rather than to serve people and bring honor to God. We'll look at these in turn. For now, let's note the dangers and have the courage to ask a few questions of our own hearts.

Here are some warning signs that you could be in danger of preaching idolatry:

You can never read the Bible for your own soul's profit. It just doesn't seem important anymore. Now you're consumed with studying the Bible for the sake of others. In fact, when you do sit down to read your Bible, you actually start noting how you could preach the passage, and you're halfway through preparing an outline before you realize it. Maybe your soul is starting to shrivel just as your work expands.

You can never say no to a sermon. You get restless when you're not preaching on a Sunday. You struggle to listen to the truth of a sermon, because instead you're critiquing the sermon. You're always looking for more opportunities to preach. Called you may be, and compelled to preach—well, that's a given; but are you a preaching obsessive?

Your moods are dictated by your ministry. A great preaching experience, and you're elated. A critical comment afterward, or your own sense of failure, and you're devastated for days. Every preacher knows that he invests massively in preaching and that joy or sorrow (sometimes mixed together) will always come, along with exhaustion. But watch those reactions. Your emotions may tell you much about whether your preaching is a service to others or a way to serve your own felt needs.

The call to preach is a call to guard against idolatry in your heart, not just to preach against it in your pulpit. It is a call to love Jesus Christ.

24

Our Honor or His?

Q. What does the third commandment teach us?
A. You shall honor the name of God as you preach.

———

You shall not take the name of the LORD your God in vain.
Exodus 20:7

The tongue. That mayhem-working muscle, which mixes praises with cursing and criticism, encouragement and blessing with blasphemy, all in a single day (sometimes a few minutes). God deliver us from what our hearts want, and what our tongues speak, when his honor is at stake.

God's name is who God is. In our thoughts or words, God is never just a three-letter idea. He is who he has declared himself to be in Christ. If we don't stir ourselves up and fix ourselves on who God is as we pray to him, or preach him, aren't we just lifting up our souls to an idol (Ps. 24:4)? Our thoughts and our words must honor God in his self-declaration. Anything less is blasphemy.

To honor God's name means to love him. Adam in the garden was called to love God by living in the light of who God declared himself to be. Instead, Adam took the easy way of immediate sense gratification, and the empty promise of having God's power for himself. In another garden, Jesus refused to go the easy way of saving himself from what he knew would be the agony of the cross. He honored God's name by taking holy wrath directed at unholy sinners by becoming sin for them. Honoring isn't easy, nor is it an option.

Preachers must honor God. That much is obvious. As most preachers soon discover, staying true to God and loving him when it's hard and brings conflict can feel like agony. A friend recently went through a really tough season in his ministry and lost so much weight that his mother thought he had cancer. Other friends have been burned out and had to step back from ministry. Sometimes that was due to their sin, but very often it was the pressures that others' sin brought upon them. Don't pity yourself, preacher, and don't make others feel sorry for you, but do be realistic about the cost.

Calvin gives a probing warning into ways in which we (especially preachers) can break this commandment. He says, "We should not rashly or perversely abuse his Holy Word and worshipful mysteries either for the sake of our own ambition, or greed, or amusement."[1] Each danger is so real and needs thinking through.

Ambition. Sinful ambition takes many forms in preaching ministry. What is yours? Most of us don't want to be globe-trotting preaching superstars, yet how real is the temptation to crave the approval of our peer groups, or churches, or families through our preaching? No. Honor is due to the Lord. Alone.

Greed. Career preachers can gradually become money-driven preachers. I say "gradually" because few start off with that ambition. But given enough years, enough setbacks, enough envy of better-off friends, and the seeds of material greed can germinate

---

1. John Calvin, *Institutes of the Christian Religion*, ed. John T. McNeill, trans. Ford Lewis Battles (London: SCM Press, 1959), 2.8.22.

into choking weeds. Tragically, all too few preachers have the same sacrificial zeal they had when they first set out.

Amusement. Preaching demands discipline. Disciplined prepping, praying, and keeping on going through hard times are essential for a fruitful ministry. So often we want things to be fun and exciting. Adrenaline is the preacher's help when serving the Word, of course; but if you're seeking adrenaline in itself, then you're seeking your own amusement. Take up kayaking or mountain biking, anything that delivers the buzz you're seeking; but never go to the pulpit for your kicks.

Are you willing to say hard things? God is not like us, and he says things we don't like. Preachers must declare the whole counsel of God (Acts 20:27), the parts of Scripture people love and feel they understand, as well as the bewildering parts they would rather ignore. Correction and rebuke have an apostolic pedigree and mandate to them (2 Tim. 4:2). Honoring God means declaring all that he has said.

Are you willing to be unspectacular and unnoticed? Unspectacular does not equal dull. Dull preachers must learn to communicate God's Word engagingly, or must work out what they have been called to do, which actually might not be preaching. But none of us is called to unholy attention seeking. Are you a pulpit show-off? Do you like leaving the whiff of your personality, rather than the aroma of Christ? Are you willing to preach where the congregations are small and "unstrategic"? More than that, could you give your life's ministry to an unremarkable place, to pursue what might be an unnoticed ministry?

Are you willing to work hard for the sake of Christ? If your preaching hasn't brought you to your knees and left you feeling broken, you've either not been preaching long enough or not giving enough of yourself to the work. Jeremiah 48:10 makes for uncomfortable reading: "Cursed is he who does the work of the

Lord with slackness." Preaching, whether full-time or not, remunerated or done for free, is work. Often delightful, sometimes appreciated, but work, nonetheless. In this work we dare not be lazy.

God is seeking his own honor through your ministry of bringing sinners to his Son. And your honor? It's to declare the greatness of our God. One day, when we lay down this magnificent task, may God give us the grace to say, "We are unworthy servants; we have only done what is our duty" (Luke 17:10), and may we be overawed—then and now—with the privilege of serving his glory.

As Calvin says, "Whatever our mind conceives of God, whatever our tongue utters, should savor of his excellence, match the loftiness of his sacred name, and lastly, serve to glorify his greatness."[2]

2. Calvin, *Institutes*, 2.8.22.

25

Stop!

Q. What does the fourth commandment teach us?
A. You shall rest from finding your justification in your preaching, and rest content and safe in the finished work of the living Word of God, Jesus Christ.

————

We who have believed enter that rest.

Hebrews 4:3

Rest is not a sin. Not resting is. God commands us to rest. God promises us the blessing of rest. If only we would take him at his Word. And if only we would fight our natural restlessness as preachers. In our highs and our lows, we need to put aside our preaching and our prep, and just stop.

But do we know how to? Take two scenarios—one low, one high—that are part of every preacher's experience.

Your sermon was the worst one to date. Or at least, that's what last night's tossing and turning seems to tell you this Monday morning. It was dull, deadly, and a huge disappointment to you and, you're sure, to others. And it's killing you.

We all preach those killer sermons of the wrong sort from time to time. But we also sometimes hit the highs and preach excellent sermons, where the Spirit is clearly at work, and we and our hearers feel the power of God and know deepening joy in Christ. Those sermons stay in our minds, as they should. Sometimes, perhaps without our knowing it, the memory of them drives us on to an even more frenetic preaching ministry, as we push ourselves even harder to hit those heights. And that brings its own exhaustion.

Is this the world you live in? And then there's the fact that some other people rarely feel that we're doing "proper work" in preaching ministry. If you're in the secular workplace, your Sunday preaching in their eyes is your weekend hobby, equivalent to their windsurfing or their football in the park. If you're a pastor, then few will comprehend that Sunday really is a day of work, let alone that it's an exhausting one. Preaching is work, though, and very demanding work at that.

Many people, preachers included, like to be thought of as driven. Most preachers drive themselves. This is good but can also be terribly bad. The great pioneer missionary to the Muslim world Henry Martin (1781–1812) once said, "Let me burn out for God," and tragically received his wish. Driving yourself in ministry can be marriage ending, ministry ending, and health shattering. Burnout is not the will of the Lord; it is the strategy of Satan.

Rest. Stop. Even if it's the hardest thing you do in your week, have a day off, and do no work on it. The Sabbath is God's covenant gift and command to the church today. As preaching takes your Sunday energies, you'll need to find a different day to rest. Guard time for your spouse and family, if you're blessed with them. Maintain and develop good friendships. Take vacations. Take up whatever hobby or activity gets you out of the house and out of the ministry hothouse. If you are in full-time ministry, broach the subject of a sabbatical with your fellow leaders, an extended time when you can have a change of pace, scenery, priorities—whatever will rest and recharge you. Stay sane, live a normal life. As you rest, you recover from stress and pressure. Rest is a gift from heaven. Be a human being. God rather likes it when you act like a human being.[1]

There is a misstep to be aware of. Vacations will relax you and allow your mind and body to recharge. But even the longest and most exotic vacations won't cure your preaching insecurities. They reflect a spiritual neurosis. It needs the work of the gospel to help you address why you are looking for your approval—your justification—in your preaching.

The best thing many of us preachers can do for ourselves is to confess that we are insecure, and that our ministry exposes those insecurities and explains the temptation to drive ourselves. We wilt when we hear of a great ministry down the road, and we collapse when we field criticism. But probably the fiercest, most devastating voice you'll hear is the one speaking inside your head. It's you. You hound yourself because you're never good enough for you. Is that something you're willing to admit?

Don't think that this struggle is just a mental or even a private one. It goes to your heart, to your life as a disciple and a child of God. It's a struggle that exposes whether you truly believe in the gospel of Jesus Christ. How you feel about your call to preach tells you everything about how you feel about the gospel, and how deeply you're believing it.

In three brief points, here is the justifying gospel for the preacher. In this gospel we can truly rest.

1. Jesus worked at the cross to give us the promised rest of sins forgiven and heaven opened up to believers. Jesus sweated and writhed on the cross, fought for breath, and bled out his life in order to save us. He did that for godless wasters as well as for God-serving preachers.

---

1. For an accessible and practical treatment of this subject, see Christopher Ash, *Zeal without Burnout: Seven Keys to a Lifelong Ministry of Sustainable Sacrifice* (n.p.: The Good Book Company, 2016). David Murray's outstanding *Reset: Living a Grace-Paced Life in a Burnout Culture* (Wheaton, IL: Crossway, 2017) is the best book I know in this area.

He achieved for us all that we could never achieve, and never will. "It is finished" (John 19:30) is the declaration of perfection. The cross speaks peace and brings rest in the forgiveness of all of our sins. "We who have believed enter that rest" (Heb. 4:3), the very rest in God's love and favor that nothing else will bring us. Jesus is Lord of the Sabbath. That means he is the Lord who commands us to find rest, and only he has worked for the rest our souls need.

2. Listen to the One who worked and died for you, and respond. Preaching can be so crushing because hearers can be cynical and hard-hearted. So can preachers, though. We forget, and sometimes refuse to believe, the very gospel that has saved us. Listen to the gospel. Listen again. Jesus says, "Come to me." Or in the words of Horatius Bonar,

> Lay down, thou weary one, lay down
> thy head upon my breast.[2]

The gospel isn't something you give to others without hearing, heeding, and staking your all on it first.

3. Your worst sermons are your salvation just as much as your best ones. In other words, you need to believe that you are joyfully accepted by the Father's love on your worst ministry days, as well as on your best. You are a justified man. The declaration "righteous" comes from the mouth of God in the power of the Spirit and on the merits of Christ.

You shall rest from finding your justification in your preaching, and rest content and safe in the finished work of the living Word of God, Jesus Christ.

As ever, help is found in the Heidelberg Catechism.

Q. 103. What does God require in the fourth commandment?

A. First, that the ministry of the gospel and the schools be maintained; and that I, especially on the sabbath, that is, on

---

2. Horatius Bonar, "I Heard the Voice of Jesus Say," in *Hymns of Faith and Hope* (London: Nisbet, 1866), 107.

the day of rest, diligently frequent the church of God, to hear his word, to use the sacraments, publicly to call upon the Lord, and contribute to the relief of the poor. Secondly, that all the days of my life I cease from my evil works, and yield myself to the Lord, to work by his Holy Spirit in me: and thus begin in this life the eternal sabbath.[3]

Its message for preachers? It says that we are to enjoy our Sundays, not as anxious performers but as Christ-satisfied disciples. We give ourselves to God in worship and to our church families in fellowship. And we refuse to try to justify ourselves by our preaching. We yield to Jesus, surrender to his righteousness, and rest in his love.

---

3. *Our Faith: Ecumenical Creeds, Reformed Confessions, and Other Resources* (Grand Rapids: MI: Faith Alive Christian Resources, 2013), 107.

26

Respect

Q. What does the fifth commandment teach us?
A. You shall honor those who preached the Word of God to you, and obey what they taught you.

———

Remember your leaders, who spoke to you the Word of God.
Hebrews 13:7

Mum and Dad matter. Whoever brought you up, however massive their failures may have been, they need to be respected. Failure to respect our parents, whether they're believers or not, is an act of disobedience that is a denial of our gospel faith. That's what the fifth commandment effectively teaches us (cf. 1 Tim. 5:8 if you need this spelled out). God's law and gospel are given to teach and empower us to give respect where it's due. It's not easy, but it's essential.

It's not just the home where the fifth commandment must be heard and obeyed. The command sets a trajectory far beyond the home for our discipleship to follow. Wherever there is God-given authority in the home, society, and church, there God expects us to work out respect. Tax returns, speed limits on the roads, and a myriad of others laws are there as opportunities for us to show how we love Jesus by honoring the rules of the world in which he's placed us.

How are you doing, then? *Respect* is a cheap word and a costly action. Everyone wants to be respected, but all of us struggle to show respect.

Preachers quickly learn that respect is slow to come by. We are an insecure breed. We fret over what people think about our ministries, and about us. We get down over the smallest signs of disrespect (real or imagined) and obsess over whether our listeners really like us. Some Christians are locked into a spiritual adolescence. They make a show of doing their own thing and feel they have a right to it. They never get properly engaged in church life, and avoid the authority of the church's leaders. Sometimes this is by using subtle evasion tactics, and sometimes it's through obviously defiant behavior. Like many teenagers, they are convinced that they're cool, but the Word of God has a different estimation: they're just desperately immature and in need of loving help. Preachers need to find ways of bringing careful confrontation. It is a great day of spiritual progress when believers start to understand their calling to respect those who speak the Word of God to them, and to work out ways of doing it.

Rather than waiting to be respected (which is never taught in the Bible), preachers need to work out how to give honor as they should. There is no such thing as a self-made preacher. We are all products of our environment, whether influences in our current ministry or the shaping factors in our early stages of Christian growth. All of us have been deeply influenced by other preachers. Some are now in glory, many of whom, known to us only through their books, have been there for centuries; and others we will never meet, though their ministries continue to bless us through sermons we download. These men have been greatly used by God in our lives.

Honor them. That is a way you obey the fifth commandment. Be grateful to God for your spiritual fathers and ministry mentors. Learn from them, both from what they say and from how they say it. Discern their weaknesses, as every preacher has them, and don't copy them. In fact, be careful that you don't parrot your favorite preachers. They are they and you are you, and God is waiting for his truth to find expression through your own personality.

Honor the preachers who are in your life, too. The best and most godly preachers seek out others who share their calling. There's no competition or jockeying for attention. Godly preachers serve each other with support and advice, when requested. Preachers who avoid local brothers engaged in the same work show an integrity gap: who wouldn't want to support and be supported by brother preachers? Where is the honoring in avoidance?

Church members live in a secular environment of disrespect. Backbiting, disloyalty, and worse are the everyday hazards of their workplace. When they come to church, they must discover the freedom and peace of being in an utterly different culture. Respect and honor must be the tone of all relationships in the body of Christ. So it is with the preacher. The preacher who craves affirmation is an immature man who needs to go deeper into the gospel of unconditional acceptance. Just so, the preacher must work out his honoring of others, whether the church's leaders or, the most awkward, a game-playing member of the flock. As we honor those in authority, we will find it increasingly easy to honor those with no authority.

As we do this, our discovery will be that our Lord has done just the same before us. The One who always honored his parents gave himself for the prostitute and tax collector. He also handed himself over to the authorities who would take his life. That is obedience to the fifth commandment. It will take you to the most costly places. It will honor God, though, and many will be blessed and encouraged by your obedience.

27

Servant-Hearted Servants

Q. What does the sixth commandment teach us?
A. You shall not use your ministry to harm in any way.

———

If I . . . have not love, I am nothing.

1 Corinthians 13:2

There was a murderer in my church. The regulars knew that this man (quiet, middle-aged) had been in prison, and they felt it wasn't their place to ask what he had served time for. You wouldn't, would you? Only the elders knew. So there he was, regular on Sundays, sharing a pew with the respectable and the upright. A murderer sitting next to fellow murderers.

At least, that's what Jesus says. He teaches us that we break the sixth commandment when we allow hate into our hearts, in the place of love. When we form cruel thoughts and maybe share them in cruel words, then we are committing murder (Matt. 5:21–23). His beloved disciple says just the same thing: "Everyone who hates his brother is a murderer, and you know that no murderer has eternal life abiding in him" (1 John 3:15).

The pew's not safe, and neither is the pulpit. We preachers can just as easily break the commandment by preaching out of an unloving heart and with selfish purposes.

Remember the Corinthians? This church was full of people who were very confident in the gifts they had, but they were losing sight of the reasons they had been given those gifts. They had lost sight of the primary motivation of love in the use of their gifts. Like us, they wanted to know the Spirit's power. They'd been given gifts for ministry and wanted to exercise them. But the apostle Paul saw that it could all come crashing down on their heads. His strong warnings in 1 Corinthians 13, as well as his picture of true, serving love, have rescued many a preacher. Let's dwell on this brilliant chapter, under four headings:

1. *Loveless gifts are a spectacular show.* Tongues? Wow! Prophecy? The same. Many want obvious, attention-grabbing gifts. Those of us preachers who don't seek these gifts, or who are skeptical about their so-called manifestations today, still want to be powerful preachers. Like the Corinthians, we all want a mighty mountain-shifting faith. Well, these gifts are all useless without love, Paul warns us (vv. 1–2).The most gifted can be the cruelest, relentlessly pursuing their "ministries" but utterly neglecting the real needs of those they were called to serve.

2. *Sacrifice stinks.* You can bleed for others. But you might just be shedding your blood out of a sense of duty, an iron will, or in the hope of gaining something for yourself, whether from God or anyone else. We preachers love to serve, and most of us are happy to work hard in our ministries. And therein lies the danger. Without love, we're fakes, and our efforts are a mistake (v. 3). Sacrifice is essential for an authentic preaching ministry, but sacrifice never justifies a ministry.

3. *Love looks like this.* The church can be a poisoned pond, sometimes, can't it? It is all the more depressing when we remember

that the church is the dwelling place of the Lord, by his Spirit. And yet, is it full of people who are, well, just like us at our worst. That is why Paul lists the attributes of love. In doing so he doesn't write a pretty poem; he instead describes tough qualities that are the antidote to our poisonous attitudes and habits (vv. 4–7). We must reflect on them, repent over them, and pray them into our lives. Then, by grace, we work out how to live with the new attitudes and habits of a life well lived, a life of love.

Impatient Christians. Ruthless Christians. Squabbling Christians. Self-promoting Christians. Self-satisfied Christians. Touchy Christians. Score-settling Christians. Unforgiving Christians. Now substitute the word *preachers* for *Christians* in that list. It sounds rather harsh, doesn't it? Most of us don't speak about sin in the pulpit without a painful awareness of our own. We pray for patience with our more difficult listeners, and we try to grow in loving them. But we can still harbor a whole array of sins in our hearts, or be contented that we don't display in our lives the grosser sins we see around us. May the Lord humble us and convince us that he wants nothing less than the radiance of Jesus in our daily living.

4. Love lasts; church stuff doesn't. Love is the life of heaven lived on earth. Love, like heaven, is permanent. The spectacular gifts will fade one day (v. 8). One day all will be revealed, and there will be no need for tongues and prophecies (vv. 9–10), or for sermons and preachers. One day we will all finally grow up and put our childish ways behind us, chief among them the desire to be noticed and thought well of (v. 11). One day we will see Jesus, and we will think and make much of him. After all, we walk by faith, not by sight, even sight in the precious gifts to be shared in the body of Christ. Be content to believe, content to hope, and serious about love. Those who out-love this world will also outlive it.

28

Faithful Attraction

Q. What does the seventh commandment teach us?
A. You shall not be unfaithful to your ministry by failing to love those you preach to.

———

You shall not commit adultery.
Exodus 20:14

We never meant to do it. Of all people, we were the ones called to preach. It was only yesterday when we were overwhelmed with excitement. We were in love. We were in love because we were loved. God had brought us to his Son, and then, in his timing and by his providence, he called us to the ministry of preaching. How thrilled we were! We could hardly believe that we were the ones walking to the pulpit and how eager we were to preach to this dear group of people. Our hearts could almost burst. Why this call to us to preach?

We never meant to do it. Our love stumbled. We thought this love of declaring God's truth to his people would last forever. Then came disappointment. Someone didn't like the sermon (or the illustration, or us), and after they didn't like it for the tenth time, we wondered if we liked them anyway. After the thirtieth time, and then the hundredth, our love cooled, our eyes wandered, our hearts questioned. Did we really need to serve this people, in this way, at this cost? Weren't we, of all people, above this? Adultery was knocking at the door, and calling through it.

Preachers are tempted to commit adultery. Obviously that means the full-on David and Bathsheba kind, a man and a woman breaking of their marriage covenant, thus destroying themselves and those they have loved. I've seen this wreckage at close quarters. And then there is the cut-your-own-throat adultery of pornography. Preaching friends of mine have shared, out of deep self-loathing, the snare that porn has been to them and the harm it's caused their ministries, marriages, and walks with the Lord. Adultery is death for everyone involved.

But there is a clean-hands and pure-bodies adultery that no one sees and is seldom confessed or even recognized. And that is the preacher's heart-lust for Something Else. Something Else? It's that congregation, that situation, that success, that appreciation (and maybe that wage) which we don't currently have. Whether Something Else is a real person or place, or just an imagined one, a preacher's temptation is to take his heart's love from what God has given him and to set it on what he believes he is entitled to.

We never meant to do it. But it's happened to us, and we feel helpless. Maybe we're willing captives of our feelings. We nurture them, and we reason that, because we have them, they must be right—and that we really must be that good at preaching to know we're entitled to Something Else.

Adultery isn't the main sin, though; doubting God's goodness is. Adultery begins with the Adam-and-Eve heart that looks at the garden of God's generous love and asks, "Is this all?" Adultery loves the self and therefore easily pities the self. Self-pity then finishes its perfect work, lusting after what God in his wisdom hasn't seen fit to give. Adultery looks at the forbidden tree and says, "I must have this." And where the heart sins, the mind and then the body will always follow.

We need to be bravely honest. When did you last spend some time just rejoicing in your gospel privileges? Have you recently thanked the Lord for the work he's called you to? Have you honestly confessed your disappointments and struggles to him, or are you holding them close and allowing them to shape a discontented, resentful heart? When all is said, do you know God as good and generous, the only heart satisfier; or have you grown cold and skeptical, fixating on what you don't have and gradually consumed with longing for it?

Brothers, we are loved. The gospel is the greatest heart affair that creation and all worlds have ever known, or will know. The gospel love of God, for his Son and for all whom the Father and Son set that love upon, is the song of heaven, the joy of almighty God, and the love we were redeemed to know in all its fullness (Eph. 3:14–19). No other love will ever outlast, outshine, or out-satisfy this one. How could it?

"Keep yourselves in the love of God" (Jude 1:21). If you are this loved through Christ, then explore it, stay in it, allow it to satisfy you.

> Keep your heart with all vigilance,
>   for from it flow the springs of life. (Prov. 4:23)

Circumstances are never the well-spring of life. Life is found in grace, and grace in a heart and mind changed by the Lord Jesus Christ and living closely to him. "The heart is the main thing in true religion, and there can be no purity of life without it," wrote Thomas Watson.[1] Guard your heart. Here are nine ways you can do that:

1. *Protect your heart with God's Word.* What are you feeding your heart? The promises, the encouragements, the warnings, the truth of God's Word are what your heart needs, every day. Don't rely on your sermon prep for your heart food.

2. *Keep a prayerful heart.* Prayer is living with God as the great reality. Bring your heart to God in prayer. Live with him, and he will fill and satisfy your heart.

---

1. Thomas Watson, *The Pure in Heart*, in *The Beatitudes* (Pensacola, FL: Chapel Library, 2008), 4.

3. *Keep a thankful heart.* Satan will tell you that God can't make you happy, that God isn't good, that God isn't enough. But open your eyes to all that God does gives you, and has given you. Be thankful. "The cheerful of heart has a continual feast" (Prov. 15:15).

4. *Guard against a complaining heart.* Complaining is spiritual poison, whether we drip it over our own hearts or we splash it over others.

> The vexation of a fool is known at once,
>   but the prudent ignores an insult. (Prov. 12:16)

5. *Watch out for a restless heart.* Restlessness brings wretchedness, quite simply. "Godliness with contentment is great gain" (1 Tim. 6:6).

6. *Keep your heart free from the love of power.* Jesus said, "One's life does not consist in the abundance of his possessions" (Luke 12:15). Many preachers (pastors especially), don't have an abundance of possessions. Our lust is to possess power and influence. They don't bring life, but usually take it.

7. *Guard your heart against sexual temptation.* Lust destroys, porn kills, sexual sin disqualifies and devastates. Hate it, and fear it.

8. *Keep your heart open to good Christian friends.* Sin craves privacy. If you're living a very private life, if you are living away from the loving accountability of a good Christian friend or friends, then please take these words seriously.

9. *Know that you alone cannot guard your heart.*

> Prone to wander, Lord, I feel it,
> prone to leave the God I love.

You cannot guard your heart alone; you're not called to.

> Here's my heart, Lord, take and seal it,
> seal it for Thy courts above.[2]

---

2. Robert Robinson, "Come, Thou Fount of Every Blessing," in *Songs for the Sanctuary: or, Hymns and Tunes for Christian Worship* (New York: Barnes, 1873), 340.

29

Give

Q. What does the eighth commandment teach us?
A. You shall not withhold your heart and soul from the hard work of preaching.

———

You shall not steal.
Exodus 20:15

Theft is the sin that other people commit, isn't it? That's the teenage boys casting shifty glances outside the news stand, eyeing up passers-by for bags, phones, or wallets. Or it's big businesses, paying farmers and manufacturers a pittance for the products they work hard to produce. And it's the failed and corrupt regimes in the Developing World and sometimes closer to home, exploiting the very people who voted them into power. It's not us, and it's certainly not the preachers among us. Right?

Don't be so confident. The sins we feel safest about usually turn out to be the ones that have us by the throat. Ask yourself, how do you spot a thief? To recognize a thief, you have to know what theft is. Theft is taking whatever does not belong to you. No surprises there. The eighth commandment is short because it's simple. Our difficulty with it is that it's so wide-ranging that none of us can actually keep it. And there's no thieving without thieves.

Money, resources, time, opportunities; and then there's the theft of emotional energy, and the theft of care other people need from us but we choose to keep to ourselves.

But thieving preachers? Sadly, yes. I know of one who actually tried to rob a bank, and a couple of others who landed in a pile of trouble for preaching someone else's sermons. Our preaching theft is more subtle and actually more damaging, because it can go on for many years without detection, least of all by ourselves. And like all crimes, theft is never victimless.

We may rob people of respect in how we preach to them. We may be arrogant, patronizing, rude, or harsh. We may rob God of his glory as we make ourselves the focus of ministry, not Jesus Christ. We may steal people's energy and time, preaching for too long and wearying them with sermons we ought to have landed five or ten minutes earlier. It's a depressingly long list.

I want to focus on one preaching sin, which is this: the sin of withholding time and energy from sermon prep instead of committing ourselves to the hard work, heart and soul. Think with me about this unnoticed but devastating misdemeanor.

Let me be clear: I love sermon prep. I love the thrill of starting each week with a passage (or two) of Scripture to go deep into. I love it, and yet—as all preachers know, and only they know—preparing for the pulpit is time-consuming and tiring. I have a postcard in my study with a line from Jane Austen on it: "How often is life destroyed by preparation, foolish preparation!" She didn't have sermon prep in mind, and the prep that we preachers must do is never foolish; but it is seemingly endless and demanding, and sometimes seems to return few rewards. I, for one, find that I am tempted to wriggle away from the discipline of sermon prep.

Giving sufficient time each week to preparing sermons is an act of will. It is a commitment to self-discipline, and when we decide to do it, it will put pressure on the rest of our schedules. It is, though, supremely an act of love. We want to serve our people to the very best of our abilities. So we work hard for them in ways they will never actually see but, we hope, will benefit them as we come to preach to them.

Stealing, of course, doesn't rule out gleaning the best insights from others for your sermon. There's no substitute for prayerfully studying the text on its own. But after that, you must consult the commentaries, chase down theological tomes, read around the subjects, evaluate the perspectives of non-Christian thinkers on the issues your text presents, and then listen to how others have preached the text. I listen to two or three sermons a week on my iPod, usually when I'm exercising or driving. If your sermon is dazzlingly original, it's probably either heretical or terrible, or both. Far better men than us have written on the Scriptures through the centuries or are preaching them today. So access them.

It's hard work, though, and when preparing is hard work, we will look to ease the burden. We might cut the prep time, recycle old material, or, if we feel we know the passage adequately, preach without notes, relying on our recall.[1] Worst of all, we might preach other people's sermons. Our Internet age means that the busy preacher is tempted to recycle Pastor Exceptional's greatest sermons. By all means, take insights into the text and ways of handling it from the best you can listen to; but the sermon must have life, and life for the preacher comes only as the Holy Spirit burns that text and its message onto your heart. If you try to get by on someone's else sermons, sooner or later you will see yourself for the fraud you've become. Don't fake it in the service of the Lord and his people.

---

1. I'm not against preaching without notes, and I do it from time to time. My observation on preaching without notes is that it (a) impresses the congregation no end (and risks becoming glory-theft, as listeners are impressed that you can do it) and (b) can be a cover for having done little rigorous work with the text. If you work hard in the study and then preach with no or few notes so that people are edified, brilliant. But note the dangers.

Paul charges the Corinthians to be "always abounding in the work of the Lord, knowing that in the Lord your labor is not in vain" (1 Cor. 15:58). That means that we must prepare our sermons carefully, in season and out of season. We fight to give our prep time the place it needs in crowded weekly planners. We discipline ourselves to resist distractions (no phone, email, or Internet checking during sermon prep time is a must). We do this hard, tiring, but vital work as our love gift for Jesus and for his people. Anything less may well be theft.

30

True to His Word

Q. What does the ninth commandment teach us?
A. You shall not say anything untrue in your ministry.

———

Rather, speaking the truth in love.
Ephesians 4:15

Lying is a beast that takes many forms: exaggerating, masking the truth, shading the truth, being economical with the truth, "misspeaking," using flattery, masking our motives, gossiping, slandering. You can probably think of others. Whatever forms lying takes, you've been hurt by them, and the chances are that you've hurt others through them. We are, by instinct and just as Isaiah confessed in God's presence, "a people of unclean lips" (Isa. 6:5).

Where Scripture gives a command in the negative—"Do not lie"—we often also hear the same command in positive form— "speaking the truth in love" (Eph. 4:15). Notice that the apostle doesn't say, "Love the truth, and then just open your mouth."

We've all felt the blasts of the eager Christian who's out to correct us and to bend us to the convictions he loves so dearly, regardless of our own views or needs. This is maybe a love of the truth, but a love of people is all too absent. Woe to the church if that is the preacher's manner. Obedience to the commandment "Do not lie" does not mean "tell the truth regardless of whom you crush under it," but it means "tell the truth in order to serve others in love."

Paul's vision in Ephesians 4:15 is for the whole church to be so taken up with Jesus Christ that its members are committed to investing in one another's lives with words that glorify Jesus and do each other good in him. Of all who speak in the church, then, the preacher especially must pursue and model this wonderful priority. There is no such thing as "naked truth" in the pulpit: truth must be ministered, and that means it must be delivered with abundant and sincere love.

Let's be clear: that does not mean we're mealy mouthed, never identifying sin for what it is. We speak the truth, always. We do that when it's uncomfortable and stressful, and when we won't be loved for doing so. We are called to make followers of Jesus Christ, not to build a personal fan base. Jesus was a man of truth, and his authentic servant will be too. "Peace, Peace, where there is no peace" sermons have a long and biblical pedigree, but they always come from the lips of false prophets, and they are always condemned (see, e.g., Jer. 6:13–15; Ezek. 13:10). Spurgeon declared,

> We might sooner pardon the assassin who stretches forth his hand under the guise of friendship, and then stabs us to the heart, than we could forgive the man who comes towards us with smooth words, telling us that he is God's ambassador, but all the while foments rebellion in our hearts, and pacifies us while we are living in revolt against the majesty of heaven.[1]

So how do we watch our hearts and then our lips as preachers? Try these three starters:

---

1. C. H. Spurgeon, "A Blast of the Trumpet against False Peace" (February 26, 1860), in *The New Park Street Pulpit*, vol. 6 (London: Passmore and Alabaster, 1860), 117.

We love the truth and the God of truth. Jesus is the true God and the eternal life (1 John 5:20). All we do is for his glory and is an expression of the life and grace that are in him. Preaching has no other goal.

But are we convinced of this? Are we captivated by the glories of God's true gospel in his Son; or are we exalting the shadow glories (sorry, the idolatries) of our own hearts? If we've forsaken the truth at these deep, personal levels, then we're living a lie. And what we live, we will speak. No pulpit is safe when an idolater stands in it.

We fear harming the body of Christ and dishonoring Christ's name before the world. Christ's bride is loved by her Savior. He knows all of her faults, and yet he loves her with a deathless love. He never lies to her, runs her down behind her back, abuses his authority over her, or uses her for his own personal gain. "Be imitators of God" (Eph. 5:1) means that we're called to this same loving integrity. Just so, Christ has invested his reputation in the church and its ministry. Dare we abuse our preaching and the people of God so that the Savior is dishonored by us?

We ransack our hearts and get rid of false ministry motives. Why are you engaged in ministry? Why did you start preaching in the first place, and what makes you keep on preaching, especially when it's hard? If you find any answers apart from a burning desire to serve Jesus Christ in bringing his gospel to others, your ministry will be in trouble. Enough disappointments, and you will start using ministry for your own gratification. Then heaven help us all.

We preachers face the temptation to use ministry to pursue personal goals. Maybe it's popularity, a craving for attention, the exciting rush of feeling that we're influencing people. Some use the pulpit as a means to financial security. Whatever your pulpit abuse, one of your first casualties will be the truth.

How so? You'll default to flattery, exaggeration, even down-right lies to achieve what you want. Your preaching will be your

156 Loving the Word

attempt to persuade others that you're clever, important, love-able, or anything else on which you're basing your identity. The truth of God, the whole truth, with Jesus at the center, will become a chore, because it doesn't achieve your appointed goals. The Word preached faithfully deeply inconveniences you as well as your hearers with its demands. Your pride won't allow that for very many years. In time, you'll preach less of the Word and more of yourself.

And so we're back where we started. "Speak the truth in love" is a command we can keep only when we're resolved to love others. If your ministry is a journey in self-love, then no one gets served, you least of all. If by grace you lay your heart and work before the King of kings, then your words will be filled with truth and love. Only then do preachers truly serve the King.

31

Resist

Q. What does the tenth commandment teach us?
A. You shall not set your heart on another's ministry and gifts.

————

You shall not covet.

Exodus 20:17

What does it mean to obey the command not to covet, when we are called to be hungry for God's power in and through our ministries? How do we obey the command to be content without being resigned to what might be a sinful ministry mediocrity? And how do we study closely the fruitful ministry of a friend, or a long-dead hero, and pray for more of his gifting for ourselves without allowing a corrosive coveting to set in?

One of the greatest psychological pressures for any preacher is being content with our current experience of God's grace and managing our longings for so much more blessing. No one said that this would be easy; but nobody told us how hard it would be to live with a preacher's heart, which both longs for God's glory and lusts after his own—or covets somebody else's.

Coveting Blasts a Ministry

"Do not covet." The commandment challenges our attitudes toward other people and toward what God has given them. Of course, it also challenges our attitudes about ourselves and how God has ordered our lives. Ministry itself offers ample fare for the envious heart. Where are the default settings of ingratitude and envy in our hearts? Do we covet what those in our churches have—their houses, salaries, cars, holidays? And then there's the preacher up the road, or on the conference platform. Why is he so blessed when we are obviously more talented (and godly)? Why does he get those invitations, and that attention, when we believe it should come our way? Why is his church, his salary, his reputation, his cult following so big?

In the world, coveting might look like power. Powerful people are always demanding more, and working and fighting to get it. In the eyes of God, though, it looks like weakness. A coveting man is restless, joyless, and wretched company for those who must endure him. The preacher might sometimes dress up his grasping ambition as "a passion for the lost" or "a zeal for Christ." He may even convince a good number that his heart is honest. The truth might be that he simply wants the buzz of more people listening to him and an enhanced reputation as a big hitter. Preachers who are always longing for more are decreasingly happy with what God has given them. Their love for the Lord cools, their impatience with his people creeps in, and their longing for anything or anywhere except their current calling eats away at them. A covetous man is actually a weak man, and a covetous preacher might be weakest of all.

The greatest weakness of coveting is usually a lack of faith.

Coveting, at root, is a refusal to recognize God as God. His Word tells you that he is wise, good, and generous. Your heart repeats the Devil's whisper that God is stingy, unloving, disinterested. The Serpent bites again, and you're left feeling "poor little me" as you look at your life and ministry. Yet again we've believed the poisonous lie, that God isn't the God of his Word, good and loving, but some selfish monster of our imagining and the Devil's suggestion. Let this lie live, and your poisoned heart will covet.

Coveting refuses to yield to the life and ministry God has ordained for us. Coveting refuses to trust in his generosity and wisdom. When you refuse to trust God in what he has given you, you are accusing God of being unloving and unwise. Coveting is evil, ugly, and dangerous.

Contentment Rescues a Heart, and a Ministry

So, how will you obey this commandment? Here are four pointers:

1. Believe that God is who he is. He is "the blessed God" (1 Tim. 1:11) meaning the God of deepest, unchangeable, and holy contentment. He is not frustrated, stressed, or brooding. He is just in all he does and loving in all of his ways (Ps. 145:17). Contented servants reflect the nature of their master.

And the contented God wills and works for your contentment. John Newton once made the stunning comment "Everything is necessary that God sends your way; nothing can be necessary that He withholds."[1] That is your life as disciple and preacher. Unbelief tells us that God has withheld the good and sent the bad, and our hearts rebel in covetous desires. They are our wretched efforts to get the good that we believe God is withholding. But we must repent of our foolish thoughts and desires. He is good, and all that he does and gives is for our best. If we don't have what we currently want, that is for our good. It is necessary. Trust him.

2. Identify your discontentment, and starve it. Where are you lusting for what is not yours? Where have you exchanged contentment in God's providence for a restless longing for what he hasn't

---

1. John Newton, "On the Right Use of the Law," letter 4 in *The Works of John Newton*, 6 vols. (Edinburgh: Banner of Truth, 1985), 1:345.

given? Be specific. Can you list the gifts, successes, circumstances, or pleasures you tell yourself you can't live without? Dare to identify them. Confess them, and ask for the Spirit's help to understand why you really want them. Ask him to show you your heart, and then to wean it from your discontentment and fix it onto his goodness in Christ.

3. List your blessings, and celebrate them.

My flesh and my heart will fail [and we could add, "so will
  my ministry"],
    but God is the strength of my heart and my portion
      forever. (Ps. 73:26)

What do we deserve from God? Nothing. All our gifts, all we have is by grace. A sense of entitlement feeds a greedy heart. But a keen awareness that we deserve nothing but have all of God's love in Christ will humble us and satisfy us. Then all of the gifts in our lives—people, circumstances, privileges, ministries (even with the tears they sometimes bring)—will be seen for what they are, stunning blessings from God to be counted up and treasured with thanksgiving.

4. Knowing Jesus is contentment.
"Godliness with contentment is great gain" (1 Tim. 6:6). The beauty of the gospel is that we don't need to covet, because we have enough. The love of God in Jesus Christ really is sufficient and satisfying. Our identity isn't in what we have or want, or in others' approval. Nor is our contentment found in success, achievements, or anything else. We were created to know peace in God's love in his Son, and the gospel both calls us and empowers us to do just that.

32

The Heart of the Law

Q. What is the summary of the Ten Commandments for preachers?
A. Loving the Lord your God and your neighbor, not your preaching, is the goal of the law.

———

"You shall love the Lord your God with all your heart and with all your soul and with all your mind and with all your strength." . . . "You shall love your neighbor as yourself."
Mark 12:30–31

A preacher approached Jesus with a question and, most likely, a point to make: "Which commandment is the most important of all?" (Mark 12:28). Jesus had been trailed by crowds hungry for wisdom, or a show, or both, and his hearers knew that he would always have something to say against their self-appointed overlords, the Pharisees.

The answer the Master gave was certainly sound—love God and love your neighbor (Mark 12:30–31). Solid and solidly orthodox theology. Moses said it (Deut. 6:4–5), and Jesus believed it, as they all did. The addition Jesus made to his answer was the knockout: "You are not far from the kingdom of God" (Mark 12:34). Jesus was basically saying, "Great theology; now make sure you believe it and live it." Having the right verse in your mind and on your tongue is not enough. Loving the God who speaks that truth and serving all who need his grace, that is our calling. Preacher, he's speaking to you.

Some things in Christian theology are very simple. A child knows that God is real, and that God is good, and that putting him first and loving others is the essence of life. You and I know that, too. But we can trip over the simple. Somehow, in the midst of our calling, we forget this simple theology, that our preaching is an act of love for God and for people. Without that love, our preaching is nothing. Worse still, we might well find ourselves far from the kingdom.

Are we called to love preaching? Take care with your answer. The question's not a trap, but it does have its dangers. It's actually not misdirected love to love preaching. If preaching is the declaring of all that God is and does through his Son, then who could not love that declaration and the call to share in it? Preaching should take our hearts' love. "I fear none of us apprehend as we ought to do the value of the preacher's office," said the Princetonian James W. Alexander.[1] That isn't a whimper of self-pity from a preacher who feels undervalued. It's an observation that if preaching is the proclamation of God's excellence in Christ, then the preacher's work is of the highest importance. We preachers must love that work.

Love always captivates, or it's not love. Preaching must capture us, and we must be driven to do our very best, dependent upon grace. Alexander continued: "To be powerful in pulpit address the preacher must be full to overflowing of his theme, effected in due measure by every truth he handles, and in full view, during

1. James W. Alexander, *Thoughts on Preaching: Being Contributions to Homiletics* (Edinburgh: Banner of Truth, 1975), 9.

his preparation and all his discourse, of the minds which he has to reach."[2] That is the language of commitment, and of committed love. All preachers will know that call to be fully taken up with the work.

Preachers are ambitious. At least, we should be. If we don't long that people will meet the risen Christ through our ministry, then what do we want to achieve through preaching? We need to root out that false godliness which wants little and is content with even less. Some reason that as long as we've preached orthodoxy, then God must be glorified. Isaiah 55:11 is quoted as the proof text of this dismal spirituality. Hearers might be left feeling empty, but our consolation—and we hope theirs, too—is that the Word will not return to God empty. But if our hearers are not presented with Christ in such a way that they are compelled to receive Christ by faith, then what has been achieved? A preacher who aims at merely saying what the Word says, with no prayerful longing that the Word would bear fruit, isn't a God-honoring servant.

The danger lurks, though. Every preacher has experienced it to different degrees. Give your heart to preaching and expect it to love you back and fulfill all of your needs, and you'll be bitterly disappointed. Preaching doesn't love anyone. You can't expect that it'll satisfy your heart. Any preacher who seeks to find his life in his pulpit ministry is kidding himself all the way to idolatry. Preaching will pass.

God and his kingdom will never fade away. God and his people always deserve and call for the love of the preacher. The lost we will always have among us, and they need our deepest love. You and I must strive for excellence as we preach, without ever losing sight of the excellence the Lord calls for: ultimately, loving him and our neighbors is all that counts. That's our highest calling, in the pulpit and out of it.

---

2. Alexander, *Preaching*, 11.

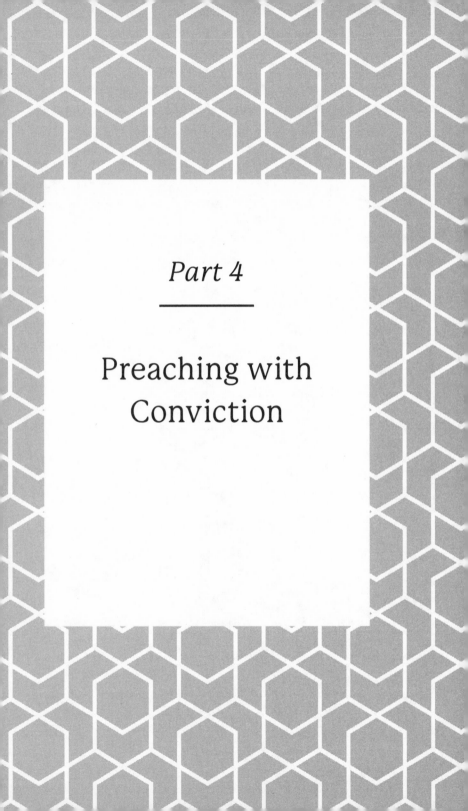

Part 4

———

Preaching with
Conviction

33

Trusting Ministry

Q. Why should we believe in our preaching?
A. Jesus offers himself through his Word in the gospel. Stand
on the rock of this truth.

————

We know that a person is not justified by works of the law
but through faith in Jesus Christ, so we also have believed in
Christ Jesus, in order to be justified by faith in Christ and not
by works of the law, because by works of the law no one will
be justified.

Galatians 2:16

Believe your own sermons. In fact, if you don't, you'll soon be in
a world of trouble. Preaching is God dealing with his world and
his people. Your pulpit dealings with your hearers are therefore
God's. He is going about his work as you are going about yours.
Jesus is offering himself through his Word as you declare it. Your
hearers must believe that, but equally, so must you.

Faith comes through hearing (Rom. 10:17). Faith is a wonderful gift of grace that the Holy Spirit gives and then sustains as we hear the Word of God. This much we believe. But the preacher sees more than enough every Sunday to make his faith shudder. Sometimes the biggest struggle going on each Sunday morning is in the preacher's heart as he fights to keep hold of his faith in the torrent of discouragement all around him.

A little reflection in a preacher's life brings back memories that are never really buried. As he's preached, he's watched people nod off into deep sleep. Others have scowled, shaking their heads almost involuntarily at a point he's made, avoiding his eyes, or avoiding him after he's preached. Others have thanked him for the sermon, only to spend the next six days doing the opposite of what he taught them. And then there's the heartache of ministry between Sundays. People are lost in the deepest pits of despair, sin, indifference, and distraction. They misunderstand the sermon or forget it altogether. One day, he fears, they might join the crowd who went down the road to enjoy the fireworks of the latest church in town—all miracles and no Bible.

I could go on, and you could add your personal horror stories, but the point is obvious: for all the real faith and spiritual growth we witness as a result of our preaching, there's so much we see that is both worrying and very discouraging. Satan delights in our discouragements, and we are tempted to wallow in them. We're tempted to lose heart in preaching. Some of us, though we go on preaching for years, already have lost heart.

Is there any way back to real confidence about the work we do?

The Westminster Shorter Catechism takes us back to first things. This is where it all began for you before even your call to preach. It began, as it must continue and as it will finish, with Jesus and faith in him. This simple, simple truth must be learned all over again. Listen to the catechism:

Q. 86. What is faith in Jesus Christ?

A. Faith in Jesus Christ is a saving grace, whereby we receive and rest upon him alone for salvation, as he is offered to us in the Gospel.[1]

Notice in the catechism that faith is a saving "grace." It is not a work. Salvation is of the Lord, and that includes the gift of faith in order to receive the saving work of Christ (Eph. 2:8; cf. 1:19). True saving faith is nothing less than the work of the Spirit of Christ in our hearts. Our own experience confirms this truth: Jesus died and was raised for us, only then to come to us in the convicting power of the Spirit, gifting us with repentance and faith. "So we have come to know and to believe the love that God has for us" (1 John 4:16).

Grace is not a safety net, needed only when our tightrope walk amid sin goes wrong. Grace does not make God a last resort when we've grown tired of sin. Grace is not something we preach to others but pass over ourselves. Grace is not for new Christians only, leaving those of us experienced in the faith to rely on effort. Grace is for preachers. Grace is for everyday living and ministering.

Grace is who God is in Jesus Christ. Outside Jesus Christ, God is wrath. The hymn says,

Foul I to the fountain fly,
wash me, Saviour, or I die.[2]

In Christ, God is gentle, saving, and strengthening love. Next time you use the word *grace*, use it with awe and thanks. It will sound, and taste, all the sweeter.

The preacher's first and last task is to live in the world of the gospel. The gospel is not only the message he offers to others; it is the gift he joyfully receives moment by moment from God. And Jesus is God's gospel. As Calvin wrote, "We enjoy Christ only as

---

1. *The Westminster Shorter Catechism* (Edinburgh: Banner of Truth, 2015), 29.
2. Augustus M. Toplady, "Rock of Ages" (1776).

we embrace Christ clad in his own promises."[3] Embracing him is the preacher's first responsibility. And then it is the next one, and the next one—every moment, every year.

This means work. Yes, grace entails work if we are to enjoy and know it. It means bringing our pain, our weariness, our cynicism to God. It means honesty with God. You may berate yourself that you experienced flashes of anger at the person who was ignoring the very application in your sermon you knew he needed. But does that achieve anything? Better still, take that anger to God. Pray for yourself and for your hearer. Pray for a spiritual breakthrough in his or her life. Pray for the same in your own. One of our biggest challenges in preaching is that we lack a deep faith that the Lord will use our preaching, whatever the appearance. We need faith.

Growing in your faith in Jesus Christ will not change your hearers. Not immediately, anyway. That's okay. Growing in your faith will change you. It will settle your anxious heart. It will silence your lips, which so easily give vent to complaints about others, complaints that speak less of your concern for them and more of a lack of faith in God's work in them. And the more you grow in the Spirit's power in response to the Word, the deeper your confidence in this Word will be, whether privately read or publicly preached.

What you preach, despite the mishaps and the disasters, is true, and you know that it's true. Jesus offers himself through his Word in the gospel. Stand on the rock of this truth.

---

3. John Calvin, *Institutes of the Christian Religion*, ed. John T. McNeill, trans. Ford Lewis Battles (London: SCM Press, 1959), 2.9.3.

34

At the Cross

Q. What happens when we preachers actually believe in Jesus?
A. A preacher living close to the cross and relying on grace is a fearsome weapon in the hands of God.

Hide your face from my sins,
  and blot out all my iniquities.
Psalm 51:9

The cross. Those two words should hush our tongues and possess our minds. "God forsaken by God," as Martin Luther used to say, is the heart of the cross.

My fear for myself and for my preaching friends is that we risk losing sight of the drama and the compelling beauty of the cross. For preachers, the cross is all too often a doctrine to get right, to preach well, to keep believing, and to share in our evangelism. All of that is right and essential. We can do all of that, though, and yet live with unmoved hearts. We can subscribe to the truth of

the cross but not be moved by it. We can understand penal sub-
stitutionary atonement, gather all its supporting verses, and even
preach it with conviction; but we must feel its truth and be gripped
by its power in our own lives.

"The cross" is apostolic shorthand. "But far be it from me to
boast except in the cross of our Lord Jesus Christ," Paul declares
(Gal. 6:14). Key terms need unpacking, and Paul is our model.
He reminds the Galatians that "it was before your eyes that Jesus
Christ was publicly portrayed as crucified" (Gal. 3:1). What Paul
means is that he made every effort to explain the cross to the
Galatians. He labored to show them that the justice and redeeming love of God worked together in those awful hours of Christ's
dereliction in order to save the elect. There was no other way. We
have no other way to God, nor do we need one. We need the cross
more than we need anything else.

We can't feed our souls with shorthand, though. We need to
work to understand more and more of the depths of the cross.
For the sake of your soul (and only then, of your preaching) give
unhurried time to those Scriptures which teach the death of Christ
for sinners. Aim to read at least one book a year about the cross.
Regularly preach sermons that explore the cross and its significance from the many different perspectives of Scripture. The central achievement of the cross should be brought to bear in every
sermon. Don't mention it as an aside, with no connection to the
sermon's flow and message; but show it to be the way to receive
and be sure of God's mercy in every season of life as we discover
God's love for us in Christ.

Be a man of the cross.

We are never more in awe of the work of Christ for us, and
then able to serve our hearers, than when we are on our knees,
confessing our need of forgiving grace in repentance. The gospel
we preach must be the gospel we consciously rely on. And what
we rely on, we love. Our greatest need, then, is a sight of our sins,
and serious repentance at the cross for them. As we bring both our
sin and our sorrow for it to the cross, we discover again the life

Jesus died to bring us. There worship flows as we see our Savior in his life-bringing glory.

Preachers must give unhurried time to meditating on the cross. Only then, as we give our hearts to thinking and feeling deeply about Jesus and his suffering death for us, do we grow in our devotion and dependence. Reflect on these words of John Owen:

> To see him who is the wisdom of God and the power of God, always beloved of the Father; to see him, I say, fear and tremble, and bow and sweat and pray and die; to see him lifted up upon the cross, and earth trembling under him, as if unable to bear his weight; and the heavens darkened over him, as if shut against his cry; and himself hanging between both, as if refused by both; and all this because our sins did meet upon him;—this of all things doth most abundantly manifest the severity of God's vindictive justice. Here, or nowhere, is it to be learned.[1]

The Westminster Shorter Catechism asks (Q. 87), "What is repentance unto life?"[2] You already know the answer, right? You're a preacher, after all. But do you realize that all your soul's health and happiness depend on your doing repentance, not just understanding it? Repentance is the life of every true Christian.

The catechism's answer to its question is this: "Repentance unto life is a saving grace, whereby a sinner, out of a true sense of his sin, and apprehension of the mercy of God in Christ, doth, with grief and hatred of his sin, turn from it unto God, with full purpose of, and endeavour after, new obedience."

When I think about my sin, I am humiliated, and perhaps no more. When I confess my sin to God, though, I am humbled. Repentance brings me back to my loving Father and fixes me in his grace at the cross. Repentance might appear to all the world to be a psychologically unhealthy throwback to a bygone age;

---

1. John Owen, *The Works of John Owen*, ed. William H. Goold, vol. 2, *On Communion with God* (Edinburgh: Banner of Truth, 1968), 85. "Vindictive" is used here in its original sense of "bringing punishment."

2. *The Westminster Shorter Catechism* (Edinburgh: Banner of Truth, 2015), 37.

but the Christian knows that without repentance, there is no life. Repentance isn't the soul wallowing in its muck (leave that to the pigs), it is the soul forsaking everything to find forgiveness and life in Jesus.

"Repentance is a grace of God's Spirit whereby a sinner is inwardly humbled and visibly reformed," wrote Thomas Watson.[3] This pithy definition contains a world of truth and life. Repentance is a gift, given by God and worked by his Spirit, as Scripture declares (Acts 11:18; Rom. 2:4; 2 Tim. 2:25). We cannot work it up in ourselves or drag it down from heaven. God must move, giving us a sight of how wretched we are in ourselves, and a confidence of how safe and loved we are in Christ. His Spirit enables us to turn from all we once loved to all that Christ is in his mercy and grace. Of course, repentance is a command of God and gives us work to do (Matt. 3:2; Acts 2:38; 17:30). Equally, as Augustine taught us, God never gives commands without giving us the grace to obey them. You really can bring your worst sins to the cross, and we preachers have many sins and much need of grace.

Commenting on Galatians 3:1, John Calvin said, "Let those who would discharge aright the ministry of the Gospel learn not merely to speak and declaim, but to penetrate into the consciences of men, to make them see Christ crucified, and feel the shedding of his blood."[4] Preachers who know their own need of Jesus can do so, and will.

---

3. Thomas Watson, *The Doctrine of Repentance* (Edinburgh: Banner of Truth, 1987), 18.
4. John Calvin, *Commentary on the Epistles of Paul to the Galatians and Ephesians*, trans. William Pringle, in *Calvin's Commentaries* (Grand Rapids, MI: Baker, 1993), 80.

35

The Courage of
Our Convictions

Q. How can we treasure preaching, even when we feel like
no one else does?
A. The Spirit can achieve whatever he wants through his
preached Word. Believe it.

———

. . . teaching them to observe all that I have commanded you.
Matthew 28:20

No true preacher lives without trouble. Every good preacher has
been criticized, sometimes fiercely, and often unfairly. One of the
best verses a preacher can take to heart is Job 5:7:

Man is born to trouble
    as the sparks fly upward.

And preacher, you are the man.

If you thought you were going to the pulpit for a quiet life, you've totally mistaken your calling. If you thought you would float home each week after the sermon, lost in a sense of God's pleasure and deeply encouraged by the appreciation of your listeners, you're disappointed now, aren't you? Yes, there are those bright and wonderful days, and we thank the Lord for them; but every servant of the Word knows that the skies over the preacher's head are sometimes cloudy, with even a chance of a little congregational thunder.

That is the way it should be if we are true to our call. "Teaching them to observe all that I have commanded you" (Matt. 28:20) is a summons to serve controversy. *Everything*, says Jesus. All the hard bits, the faith-demanding bits, the costly bits, the this-world-will-hate-you-if-you-live-like-this bits. The whole thing. Telling people to join you in the difficult life of faith and to love Jesus in every detail of their lives makes you sometimes the loneliest man in the room.

Jesus knew controversy. John did and Paul did, too. Before their sufferings, John the Baptist lost his life out of loyalty to God's Word. Let's not even start on the Old Testament prophets. Everyone who wants to preach a godly life in Christ Jesus will be persecuted.

Sometimes, and maybe especially in our current age, it's not so much the open hostility we may encounter as we preach but the cynicism or indifference we meet that gets to us most. We discharge our duty, and people stifle a yawn. We preach a message we have labored over and given ourselves to proclaiming with body and soul. They shuffle and look at the clock.

Yes, this is preaching. And don't for a fraction of a second feel that you have permission to complain. Preaching is a strange, mysterious Holy Spirit business. The message is his, the purposes are his, and the outcomes of our preaching rest with his wisdom and power. If he exalts us as we preach, or if he sovereignly allows our lives to entail ministry struggle, it is well with him. And so it must be with us.

Please understand, this is not a counsel of resignation. If our preaching is not making the impact we long for it to have, then we must take action; and as we pray, we must ask the hard questions of our ministry. As General William Booth allegedly told two discouraged preachers in his fledgling Salvation Army, "Try tears." We need to care more, love more, pray more, and work more. God loves to give results to that sort of consecrated ministry.

Whatever the reactions or apparent lack of them to our preaching, our trust must be in the goodness and power of the Lord of the Word, especially when ministry is very hard. Suffering can skew our perspective. Suffering can lead us to mistrust God, to distort our view of him, when we most need the correct picture of him.

For William Gadsby, nineteenth-century Particular Baptist pastor, the sufferings of home life were acute and set a heavy burden upon his faith and ministry. He ministered for twenty-five years while nursing his wife, who suffered with acute mental illness. He died before she did and before she gave most encouraging signs of not having lost the faith she embraced as a girl, the faith Gadsby had been so confident that the Lord would preserve in her. The strain for him, though, was at times unbearable, as her illness led her to erratic and destructive behavior, including attacking her husband and burning his letters and sermon notes. In all his anguish, Gadsby was determined not just to preach his Master but to trust him, and to trust him more deeply, the deeper the trials. He wrote:

> I want a faith that can fully credit contradictions, and that can prove the darkest night to be perfectly light, and the greatest of trials to be perfectly right, and to be evidences of unbounded love. Yea, I want a faith that can fully rely upon a promise with a rational prospect of the promise being fulfilled. . . . I thirst, pant, and groan, for the faith of which Christ is the Author and Finisher.[1]

---

1. Cited in Ian J. Shaw, *William Gadsby* (Darlington: Evangelical Press, 2013), 80.

Your faith must embrace light and dark, triumph and disaster in your ministry. Your faith must "fully credit contradictions," the gushing thank-you texts as well as the sharp criticisms of the very same sermon. All the time you thought you were serving a ministry of encouraging faith in others. Now you recognize that you're called to grow in faith yourself, often despite what you see. This is what is involved in teaching others to obey everything Jesus has commanded you to say to them. Without your own active, growing faith, it is impossible for you to please God (Heb. 11:6), and impossible to urge your hearers to live lives of obedience either.

So, what does the gospel say to us struggling preachers? It says that we are safe, safe in God's grace. His covenant love saves and protects us. His love is always for us, his plans are always good. And his sovereignty, sometimes overwhelming as it is in the trials we face, is good and sweet.

Spurgeon, who struggled with depression for huge spells of his adult life, knew where to place his trust when life was miserable.

> There is, in contemplating Christ, a balm for every wound; in musing on the Father, there is a quietus for every grief; and in the influence of the Holy Ghost, there is a balsam for every sore. Would you lose your sorrows? Would you drown your cares? Then go, plunge yourself in the Godhead's deepest sea; be lost in his immensity; and you shall come forth as from a couch of rest, refreshed and invigorated. I know nothing which can so comfort the soul; so calm the swelling billows of grief and sorrow; so speak peace to the winds of trial, as a devout musing upon the subject of the Godhead.[2]

This is true because God is true and he is sovereign. In Jesus you really can trust him. So do.

---

2. C. H. Spurgeon, *The New Park Street Pulpit Sermons*, 6 vols. (London: Passmore & Alabaster, 1855–1860), 1:1.

36

Ministering Sacraments

Q. Will we let the sacraments preach?
A. Baptism and the Lord's Supper preach in ways we can't, and that's their very purpose.

———

He received the sign of circumcision as a seal of the righteousness that he had by faith while he was still uncircumcised.
Romans 4:11

The Westminster Shorter Catechism states that the sacraments of baptism and the Lord's Supper are given in order to represent Christ and the benefits of the new covenant, and to seal and apply Christ and the benefits of the new covenant. Or, if you will, they show you what the gospel is, and they strengthen your faith in the gospel. These are wonderful gifts of grace.

God's Old Testament people were given circumcision as a sign of his grace (Rom. 4:11), declaring to them that the covenant Lord was claiming ownership of his people, as well as teaching them of their need of a new heart (Gen. 17:9–14). As partakers in that covenant, the whole community was called to share the Passover (Ex. 12:1–27).

God's people today are commanded to show the same obedience. We receive baptism as a sign of belonging to the triune God through Christ (Matt. 28:19), with a new heart and a conscience made clean through the blood of Christ (1 Pet. 3:21). As members of this covenant family, we eat bread and drink wine, celebrating all that Christ has done for us, and proclaiming the gospel to one another, as well as to a lost world (1 Cor. 11:26).

These signs are powerful, and their message, when clearly explained and brought to our hearts by the Spirit of God, is compelling.

John Calvin's treatment of the sacraments is essential reading.[1] God, he explains, gives baptism and the Lord's Supper as props for weak faith, and as "exercises which makes us more certain of the trustworthiness of God's Word."[2] The sacraments have been "instituted by the Lord to the end that they may serve to establish and increase faith."[3] Without the Spirit's working they are empty, but with his power they are effective for his purposes.

Where did we go wrong, that we preachers have so undervalued the Lord's Supper and baptism? A glance around evangelical churches shows that the sacraments are the church's Cinderellas— tolerated, patronized, and even put to work, but little loved and even less gloried in. We love to celebrate a baptism and share the joy of grace in a person's life; but do we teach the saints to live in the light of their baptism, and to draw strength from the fact that they bear the name of the Trinity? And are our Supper services more obligation than celebration, something we would feel embarrassed to leave out of our worship, rather than something we love to share together?

---

1. John Calvin, *Institutes of the Christian Religion*, ed. John T. McNeill, trans. Ford Lewis Battles (London: SCM Press, 1959), 4.14.
2. Calvin, *Institutes*, 4.14.6.
3. Calvin, *Institutes*, 4.14.9.

In my own UK context, the rediscovery of expository preaching ministry in recent decades has taken center stage in the church. That's a great thing. We believe, in line with the sixteenth-century Reformers, that the Word gives birth to the church, and we know that the Word nourishes faith. But the Word does not nourish faith in some isolated way. The Reformers knew well, and Calvin has told us, that God has pledged to know and be known by his elect through baptism and the Lord's Supper. Through these signs he declares his covenant love and calls us to receive it.

We must also recover our belief, then, that the pulpit needs to share its message with the baptistery and the Table, and that they must be given their rightful places in the drama of redeeming grace. The sacraments are God's appointed preachers, too, and God has given them in order to proclaim Christ to us.

Let's propose a recovery. If the people of God are to find their Savior as they celebrate baptism and the Lord's Supper, then those of us called to lead churches and to preach must find a new conviction and a fresh courage.

We need *conviction* that the sacraments are gifts of Christ. God's people need them. They need the Christ who comes to them by water, bread, and wine. Our preaching must teach them and lift their expectations of receiving Christ as we participate in the sacraments. And we must participate often together.

Also, our conviction must extend to our views on preaching. Preaching is the great act of Christian worship, and it is the supreme place in which God shows himself. But the sacraments remind us that it is not the only place. If your preaching is mediocre at times, or worse than that, don't indulge in despair: the Lord is near in his sacraments.

We need *courage* to teach what baptism and the Lord's Table mean, and the courage to teach what they don't mean. We need to be brave as we handle the sacraments, making distinctions as to whom they are for and whom they are not for. Jesus doesn't teach us to open his gospel signs to anyone who likes the idea of receiving them. The Danish philosopher Søren Kierkegaard said of Jesus, "His whole life on earth, from beginning to end, was destined solely to have followers, and to make admirers impossible."[4] The baptistery and Table are to be marked, "Followers only."

Sacraments aren't for admiring fans of religion but are for the followers of Jesus alone. John Calvin once flung his arms around the bread and wine to keep them from hard-hearted unbelievers who insisted that they could receive them. Robert Murray M'Cheyne told a friend that at the Communion service he "fenced the tables from 'Christ's eyes of flame.'"[5] Are you prepared to preach the message of the sacraments, and to explain whom they are and are not for, come what may? The purity of the church and gospel, and the honor of Christ are at stake.

The sacraments are to show us the gospel and to strengthen our gospel faith, as we've seen. They teach us who belongs to Christ and who doesn't. And so, they call us to renewed trust in Christ and to enduring obedience to him, by his grace. We have been washed by Christ, and we are feeding on him. Could we need anything else?

So finish your sermon on time, preacher. Don't weary your hearers. They've heard the gospel from you. And now, in water, bread, and wine, let them see it and celebrate it.

---

4. Cited in *Bread and Wine: Readings for Lent and Easter* (Maryknoll, NY: Orbis, 2012), 55.
5. Andrew Bonar, ed., *Memoir and Remains of Robert Murray M'Cheyne* (Edinburgh: Banner of Truth, 1984), 81.

37

Take Them to the Water

Q. Why do we celebrate baptism?
A. When we honor God's command, we show its grace.

———

We were buried therefore with him by baptism into death, in order that, just as Christ was raised from the dead by the glory of the Father, we too might walk in newness of life.

Romans 6:4

Baptism is such a precious gift in our rootless, drifting age. People put on and put off different identities, and search for belonging—or resolutely refuse to belong to anything or anyone. Secularism promises a world of endless possibilities; but for those who drink deeply of its values, it's endlessly disappointing. We need more.

Baptism is the sign of entry into a new world, the kingdom that God rules through his Son. To be a baptized person is to find that your life has been caught up into the glories of this kingdom. To enter the water of baptism is to hear the declaration that God in

Christ is for you and has brought you to himself for freedom and service. Baptism is, literally, life.

Question 94 of the Westminster Shorter Catechism says that baptism "signifies and seals our ingrafting into Christ, and partaking of the benefits of the covenant of grace, and our engagement to be the Lord's."[1]

Baptism Is a Pledge of Belonging

Through baptism God says "mine!" of the person coming to the water. Baptism declares that, through saving grace, forgiveness has come, and sinners are made saints. Loved and chosen by the Father, savingly united to Christ, indwelt by the Spirit, we belong to God the Trinity. Baptism declares that truth (Matt. 28:19). Through baptism we know the delight of the Father as we submit to his command. What wonderful good news to a lonely world! The misery of exile from God has been replaced by the welcome of God. We belong to God, and he belongs to us. In baptism we have come home.

And we have come home to the family of God, the church. A private, undeclared profession of faith is as unthinkable as a private baptism is. It is suspect at best, eternally dangerous at worst (Matt. 10:32–33). Baptism is the church's celebration of covenant grace. The church belongs to us, and we belong to the church. Baptism tells us so. It's the public declaration that the Spirit has engrafted us into the people of God, and there is no salvation except that which is shared and lived out among God's people (1 Cor. 12:12–13).

We preachers need to make much of this last distinctive. In baptism both the new believer and the church recognize that they belong to each other in the one body. All good churches do baptism preparation classes with new believers. Surely we must give pulpit time to doing the same with the congregation, reminding them that baptism pledges them to all believers, old as well as new.

---

1. *The Westminster Shorter Catechism* (Edinburgh: Banner of Truth, 2015), 40.

Baptism Is the Surrender of Faith

Baptism declares, "God wins." His Word is true and he is Lord. Our sins deserve the wrath of God, death now and in the hereafter. Jesus Christ took that death in our place, dying for us at the cross. Baptism is our "coming clean": we admit that we deserve condemnation, and refuse to hide any longer before a holy God. We confess our sins, run to Christ, and are made clean by his blood.

Conversion is surrender, as surely as the Lord Jesus surrendered himself to God's will, the baptism of his suffering and death. Baptism is the same. We surrender ourselves to the water, an act that declares our death to sin and self. We identify with the Lord Jesus Christ and confess our union with him, by grace. God the Father has placed us exactly with Christ, so that the death he underwent on the cross is the death we have undergone. No, we weren't paying for our sin; Jesus alone did that. But we died there. "I have been crucified with Christ. It is no longer I who live, but Christ who lives in me" (Gal. 2:20). "We have concluded this: that one has died for all, therefore all have died" (2 Cor. 5:14). Jesus died, and if we are united to him, we have died, too. "Do you not know that all of us who have been baptized into Christ Jesus were baptized into his death?" (Rom. 6:3). Baptism is death, by grace.

With death comes life. In this surrender we come to the Lord of life. Just as our Savior was not abandoned to his grave, we rise in him to know joy in his presence and the foretaste of eternal pleasures (Ps. 16:10–11; cf. Acts 2:27–36). The surrender brings life as we follow Christ in fellowship with others.

Baptism Is Our Declaration of Holy War

The gospel is war. In the gospel God declares that he is against the world in its godlessness and will one day destroy all its disobedience. The gospel message is equally the claim that God has fought and conquered the sin and condemnation of all who come to find peace in Jesus Christ. Baptism is a swapping of allegiance, a changing of sides, so that Christ is our Captain. The baptistery is the place where we acknowledge that "we died to sin," and ask ourselves, "How can we who died to sin still live in it?" (Rom. 6:2). We have clothed ourselves with Christ in baptism (Gal. 3:27); now we follow in his footsteps, fighting, suffering, and rejoicing in his name.

John Owen once famously lamented, "Unacquaintedness with our mercies, our privileges, is our sin as well as our trouble."[2] He's right, of course. Baptism is a new world of privilege. Preachers, we must teach all that baptism is in the purposes of God, and all the grace that is set forth in it. To be a baptized follower of Jesus is, in a word, everything.

---

2. John Owen, *The Works of John Owen*, ed. William H. Goold, vol. 2, *On Communion with God* (Edinburgh: Banner of Truth, 1968), 32.

38

To Supper

Q. Why do we share the pulpit with the Lord's Supper?
A. The church tastes grace in our words and at the Lord's Table.

For I received from the Lord what I also delivered to you.
1 Corinthians 11:23

The Lord's Table is a great, great privilege for all believers. At the Table Christ preaches to us by his Spirit, proclaiming that his sacrifice is all we need for salvation, and that his abiding presence is all of our confidence for living. We hear again his promise that these signs will one day give way to the reality of his wedding supper. We taste these privileges together as the family of God. Here is living bread and the best of wine.

The family of God needs the Supper. We preachers need the Supper. Our God of words is also the Lord of signs. The signs of baptism and bread and wine are to be set before us all so that we can see our salvation and glory in our Savior. In Kevin Vanhoozer's memorable phrase, "The church is a creature of the Gospel."[1] The gospel is her true identity. Without the gospel declared and received through the preached Word and shared sacraments, she will soon be an altogether different animal.

I wonder, though; do we preachers give the Lord's Supper the attention we should? Do we trust in the power of this sign to teach worshipers about gospel realities? Or are we—people of words—tempted to push this silent Supper to the edges of God's ministry of grace? Charles Spurgeon once reflected, "I can bear my own witness that, many and many a Sabbath, when I have found but little food for my soul elsewhere, I have found it at the communion table."[2] A little humble realism might help us as we assess our preaching on Supper Sundays. It might also cause us to look to the Supper with more anticipation and thankfulness.

The truth is that we're so taken up with our preaching that often we have little time and attention left for the Lord's Table. That's literally the case. Compare your sermon prep with your Supper prep. If it takes, say, ten hours to prepare your sermon but ten minutes to select a passage to read and comment on at the Table, then which has your mind and heart? Further, when the sermon's a demanding piece of creative work to prepare (and equally demanding to deliver), and the Supper's a reenacting of someone else's story, known to all, then which will you feel more ownership of?

The odds are further stacked against the Supper when, in most evangelical traditions, the Supper comes at the end of the worship service. The end. When people are full of the Word (we hope) and naturally inclined to turn their thoughts to the rest of the day. But still we "do" the Supper. This might be with the familiar words of official or semiofficial liturgy, or with the equally well-known rhythms of so-called spontaneity and freedom. Either way, the

---

1. Kevin Vanhoozer, *Biblical Authority after Babel: Retrieving the Solas in the Spirit of a Mere Protestant Christianity* (Grand Rapids, MI: Brazos, 2016), 162.
2. Charles Spurgeon, "In Remembrance," in *Metropolitan Tabernacle Pulpit*, vol. 55, *1909* (Pasadena, TX: Pilgrim, 1979), 71.

result can be underwhelming, leaving us and the congregation feeling we've missed out on something.

We don't need novelty or experimentation as we come to the Supper. Forbid that we should tamper with the words of Christ's institution, or worse, leave them out. The Lord's Supper should be celebrated until the Lord's return, just as he ordained for us to remember his death and to seek intimacy with him, celebrating grace as his blood-bought church together. Those of us who preach on Supper Sundays and who lead at the Table have every responsibility. Mere dispensers of words and elements we are not: we must help the Lord's people, as well as the unconverted who might be with us, to see the grace set before us in bread and wine. If the Lord's Supper is for Christ's people to share gladly together, and if it is to be the focal point of their devotion, then the state of their hearts at the Table is all-important.

Take a moment and go back to those familiar words of 1 Corinthians 11:23–26. Jesus says that we are to remember him when we share bread and wine. He is to be the focus of our fellowship, the worshiping thanks of our hearts, and our hearts' trust as we eat and drink. Jesus has given himself in sacrifice for his own people. We must take the bread and cup with awe, amazed, staggered at the freeness and fullness of this grace. Is this for us? Does this grace reach even to us? Can God really lavish the life of his own Son on us? He does, he has, and he will. This bread and this wine preach to our hearts of God's astounding and overwhelming love. We eat, drink, worship, and share Jesus together, until he comes to take us to eat with him (v. 26).

Put all this together, and the preacher has work to do in a Communion service. Whatever we're preaching on, we must be aware that people will be sharing bread and wine shortly afterward. That means we are seeking to lead their minds and hearts beyond our words to the Table. A few pointers may help:

The Supper is serious. It is a solemn responsibility for individuals to share in the Lord's Supper. We don't believe that anyone and everyone should take the Lord's Supper (1 Cor. 10:21–22). Like baptism, the Lord's Supper summons us to a personal, committed discipleship to Christ. We wish to honor that in our churches.

The Supper is essentially for the church family. The Lord's Supper is a family meal, where the baptized disciples of Jesus eat and drink together. A local church is not simply a collection of people who "turn up" to activities and services (as much as we pray for and welcome all sorts of people), but a family whose members have stated their commitment to the church and to one another. So we eat our family meal in the company of each other, and as a pledge of belonging to each other, and to the Lord (1 Cor. 10:16–17).

Taking the Lord's Supper brings harm, as well as health. We want to avoid all offense, whether to believers or to non-Christians, as we share the Supper. But we want to heed Scripture's warnings about the grave danger of not recognizing the Lord and his people as we eat and drink (1 Cor. 11:27–33). For this reason we always hear a warning, before we take bread and wine, about the need to be in fellowship with the Lord and with fellow Christians. In order to share in our blessings as we eat, unconverted people as well as hard-hearted Christians need to hear that they must not expect to eat and drink without answering to the Lord for their actions. Above all, we long to share times of close fellowship with the risen Lord and with one another at the Table, full of a serious joy.

39

Seek First

Q. What is prayer?
A. Prayer is a heart open to God.

———

Go into your room and shut the door and pray to your Father who is in secret.

Matthew 6:6

I was twenty, a new Christian, and had come across the prayers of Anselm (1033–1109), one-time archbishop of Canterbury. The words below burned into my heart and mind then, and I still return to them:

Come now, little man, turn aside for a while from your daily employment, escape for a moment from the tumult of your thoughts. Put aside your weighty cares, let your burdensome distractions wait. Free yourself for a while for God and rest awhile in Him. Enter the inner chamber of your soul, shut out everything except God and that which can help you in seeking him, and when you have shut the door, seek him. Now, my whole heart, say to God, "I seek your face, Lord, it is your face I seek.[1]

Anselm wrote those famous words over nine hundred years ago as a preface to his even more famous treatise on the existence of God, the *Proslogion*. A man with many responsibilities, he knew that he needed to wrestle with his soul in order to bring it to God. He was right, and his example challenges us. If you wait until your day is less busy, your heart is less burdened, your moods make it feel exciting, or your sin takes wings and flies away, you will never pray. Although in different ways, all of us are tempted or compromised, and many of us are weary and weak in faith. Preachers are just the same. And yet, the Lord calls us to pray, as deep calling to deep. We must answer. Only as we take ourselves in hand and come to God, like Anselm, will we discover the refreshing streams of grace.[2]

Anselm's words are a response to Matthew 6:6: "But when you pray, go into your room and shut the door and pray to your Father who is in secret. And your Father who sees in secret will reward you." Jesus was speaking to people who had to deal with two main problems. He speaks to us as men who face the same twin difficulties. First, there is the daily grind of work, which takes time and saps energy. Prayer needs both time and

---

1. Anselm of Canterbury, *The Prayers and Meditations of St. Anselm*, trans. Benedicta Ward (Harmondsworth, Middlesex: Penguin, 1973), 239–40.
2. John Flavel captures the same priority and gives great counsel:

> You come reeking hot out of the world into God's presence, but you will find a tang of it in your duties. It is with the heart a few minutes since plunged in the world, now at the feet of God, just as with the sea after a storm which still continues working, muddy and disquiet, though the wind be laid and the storm over. Thy heart must have some time to settle. . . . There are few Christians can presently say, as Psalm 57:7, "O God my heart is fixed, it is fixed." O when thou goest to God in any duty, take thy heart aside and say, "O my soul, I am now addressing myself to the greatest work that ever a creature was employed about. I am going into the awful presence of God about business of everlasting moment."

John Flavel, *A Saint Indeed or, The Great Work of a Christian, Opened and Pressed*, from *Prov. 4.23*, in *The Works of John Flavel*, 6 vols. (Edinburgh: Banner of Truth, 1997), 5:464.

energy, and so daily prayer and the daily demands need to be managed together. And then there is religious hypocrisy. Those of influence in the community of Jesus's day were the ones who prayed longest, loudest, and most publicly (Matt. 6:5). Nothing changes. We preachers pray in public. Do we match that with private devotion? Do we seek intimacy with God, or applause from men? And if there is little or no personal prayer, where are the signs that we actually believe in our Father, who is unseen, and want to be with him?

As Jesus teaches, prayer is never just words. Prayer is a heart open to God. The Puritans, those men who could preach for hours and write for days, certainly knew this. The Westminster Shorter Catechism states that prayer is "an offering up of our desires unto God for things agreeable to his will, in the name of Christ, with confession of our sins, and thankful acknowledgment of his mercies."[3] Those who framed that catechism understood that prayer is never ultimately about how we sound to God, to ourselves, or to anyone else. No, in prayer we offer our hearts. God seeks nothing less.

Of course, our praying involves our words, our commitment of time, our lists, and—as the catechism states—our confession of sin and our expressing our thankfulness to God. But all this is a matter of the heart.

When we grasp this as preachers, the invitation to pray could not be more exciting, nor the dangers more real. Like all believers, we face our busyness, which crowds out prayer. "The tyranny of the urgent" is a phrase made for preachers with the constraints of sermon prep. Then there is the temptation to think that because we sound convincing in our public praying and preaching, we don't need to pray. All we can say is that the Pharisees were busy, persuasive people, and look what happened to them. Only a living, honest relationship with God nurtured and expressed in prayer, will keep us from hellish hypocrisy and fill us with the life of Christ.

---

3. Answer to Q. 98 in *The Westminster Shorter Catechism* (Edinburgh: Banner of Truth, 2015), 42.

Among preachers it seems entirely acceptable to feel guilty about our personal praying. If we were actually honest with each other, it would probably be acceptable to confess that our prayers are rushed, shallow, or even nonexistent. We have been swallowed up by the activism of our age. To pray seems weak, a cowardly retreat from the world and the work. The Spirit teaches us that prayer *is* the work. Slowly we learn. And we quickly discover that time and energy given to prayer can never be replaced by more prep or more preaching.

Prayer takes organization. Review your work patterns, your Bible reading, your devotional books, your prayer lists or apps, your sleep habits, or whatever else will help you to pray. Make time, and make yourself unavailable to others (that means your phone, too) for that time. For me, I need to have a meaningful time or prayer and reading before breakfast, and to return for a time of prayer about my ministry and those I serve before lunch. Other prayer may come at other times in the day, but if I miss those appointed slots, I feel it and my discipleship and work are poorer for it. How about you?

What happens when you open your heart to God and pray?

You care. As you pray for God's kingdom, his people, and the needs of the lost, you begin to care. God starts to work on your priorities and your compassion. You start seeing that there are people to serve with the gospel. And you start to love serving their needs.

You find you have nothing to complain about. Prayerlessness contracts your life and ministry to the size of your abilities. You'll quickly discover that those abilities, aside from grace, are tiny and feeble. And how you'll complain then! But open your heart to God, reflect on the greatness of his power and grace, and you can live with yourself and your life. More than that, you can live with contentment and peace. Only then can you bear lasting fruit.

God gets to work on your worries. When you don't pray, you get worried. Prayerlessness is abandoning ourselves either to fate or, worse, to ourselves. No wonder we find life stressful when prayer dries up. Prayer is recapturing a Christ-centered worldview, in which we celebrate again his loving rule. Problems might not go away, but they regain their God-ordained perspective.

You get refreshed. God guides you through the tasks you need to get done, and gives you strength for them. He gives you wisdom so that you don't get committed to things you shouldn't be doing or don't have the skills for. Working in his strength is joyful, fruitful, and satisfying.

Yes, our Father is unseen; but prayed-for grace is visible and glorious.

40

Praying, for His Glory

Q. Do we want God and his kingdom above all else when Sunday comes?
A. God's glory and his kingdom focus our prayers and our preaching.

———

Our Father in heaven,
hallowed by your name.
Your kingdom come.
Matthew 6:9–10

You've opened your mouth. The sermon has started, and they're listening. You have high ambitions for this time, which you've been working and praying for through the week, and you hope the congregation has, too. What are those ambitions? What do you want to achieve?

So many answers rush in when we take a moment to reflect. Yes, we have to confess that we want approval as we preach. We want people to tell us that "we smashed it" (the highest compliment a friend of mine gives my preaching). Whatever else is going wrong in our lives, we long that our preaching would be a fruitful endeavor, a bright spot in the struggle.

By grace, we have holy desires, too. We pray and long for people to encounter Christ in his Word. We long that people would grow in faith. The thought of going through the motions, ticking boxes, for us and for the listeners fills us with horror. Our hearts are usually a tangle of conflicting desires as we come to preach.

> The heart is deceitful above all things,
>   and desperately sick;
>   who can understand it? (Jer. 17:9)

We struggle to make sense of our own hearts, let alone anyone else's.

There is great and wonderful help for us, and it comes in the form of the Lord's Prayer. Jesus's lesson in prayer is for his trainee preachers (the disciples), as well as for the whole church (Luke 11:1). The prayer we are given is a call to see God, his world, and our place in it through the eyes of Christ. It is a lesson in adoration, dependence, and eager service. Preachers need it and must learn to love it.

The story is told of the time the sixteenth-century Scottish preacher Robert Bruce couldn't be found just before he was due to preach. At last, he was located in the church's bell tower, and the servant sent to fetch him reported back that Bruce was in company, as he was heard pleading, "I won't go unless you go with me." The church elders knew that Bruce's company was his Lord, and that Bruce couldn't face entering the pulpit without the Spirit's power.

You are preaching for your Father. His pleasure rests on you through his Son. The Spirit of Christ brings you to him in prayer (Rom. 8:15). Once he was the Judge who stood ready to condemn you for your sins. The Son of God died and rose again to bring you into the Father's love (John 20:17). Now he stands in love, delighting to hear your prayers and giving you his Spirit so that you can pray and be assured of his fatherly love. In fact, more than stand, we could say that the Father runs to meet us, arms outstretched, longing to embrace us as we come in our need (Luke 15:20). This is gospel love, and gospel preachers need to know it and to respond to it in prayer. You need to rest in that gospel love as you preach. The pulpit can be a very lonely place. The reassuring gospel truth is that you are never alone there.

You are preaching for his honor. The world tramples on God's name, but the church seeks to honor ("hallow") it. God's name is the expression of all that he is. The "I AM" is the exalted Lord and giver of all life. Now he is revealed in his "Christian name" of Trinity—Father, Son, and Holy Spirit—and we behold infinite truth, power, beauty, and love as we behold God. To pray that God's name would be hallowed in our preaching means that we will honor this God by declaring all that he has revealed himself to be in his Son. "Not to us, O LORD, not to us, but to your name give glory" (Ps. 115:1).

Preaching easily falls into a default setting of "Yours be the glory, O Lord; and a little to me, too, please." We need to root out that spirit of pride, that clawing, grasping, insecure longing for the praise of men. We do so with prayer. Pray that the Father would set a delight in his glory in Christ deep in your affections so that the thought of even trying to snatch a hint of the glory due God alone would disgust you. Make it your prayer that, whether you feel that the sermon goes well or not, God's name would be honored, that people would see him in Christ for who he is, the awesome one.

You are preaching for his kingdom. We pray and preach so that people will see God's glory declared in his Son. The same labor must go into helping people to embrace Christ, in whom the kingdom of God is found. If all we pray for is that people might understand God's truth—however beautiful and important that truth is—without meeting Jesus and being transformed in a relationship with him, then our prayers fall short. Our preaching will, too.

J. I. Packer says, "The Kingdom is not a place, but rather a relationship." He adds, "It exists wherever people enthrone Jesus as Lord of their lives."[1] We need to allow these words to penetrate our convictions and influence our prayers. You are praying and working not to grow a big church but to serve a church so that people will increasingly yield their lives to Jesus Christ. Whether a church of a thousand goats (or even ten thousand goatish sheep) or of ten sheep, the kingdom is displayed.

And if it needs to be said, you are not preaching for your kingdom. Preaching is not about your ministry, your reputation and influence, your success—your kingdom, in other words. The church down the road might love to exalt the Big Preacher; leave them to it. Pray that you would be content to be unknown, and apparently without any influence, as long as God is calling men and women to his Son and building his kingdom. His kingdom alone will last.

---

1. J. I. Packer, *Praying the Lord's Prayer* (Wheaton, IL: Crossway, 2007), 50.

41

Trust Issues

Q. Do we go home on a Sunday praying for God's will to be done?
A. We must pray ourselves and our hearers into a trusting contentment.

Your will be done,
    on earth as it is in heaven.
Give us this day our daily bread.
Matthew 6:10–11

What's your post-sermon meal? It might be a Sunday roast or a Sunday evening egg on toast. But what else? Do you chew on your frustrations at yourself, your listeners, or your general lot in life? Do you endlessly rerun the sermon and the conversations that followed it, picking it all apart, looking for scraps for encouragement? And then what about your conversation? Are you distant, irritable, and best left alone, or endlessly talkative after you've preached? How you think and behave after you've preached says everything about what you believe about preaching.

Many of us preachers really don't know what to do with ourselves when we get home from the sermon. We've given ourselves and made ourselves vulnerable. We've entered into a spiritual battle, facing the Devil's rage. Hours' worth of work have gone in a blur of effort, our output matched by the silence of our listeners. We're left guessing whether we've done any good. We're left exhausted by this work and overwhelmed again by its importance (and its apparent foolishness).

No one knows how draining preaching is for you, and nobody needs to. It's your burden. Others in your church have their own burdens, and if you really understood them, you'd be grateful you're spared them. Yet, this work of yours is shattering emotionally, mentally, and physically. To pray "Your will be done" involves, among other things, a willingness to be spent in God's service.

So you go home, certainly tired, maybe elated, or maybe downcast. You eat, you chat, you think. And what else?

You pray. You pray for your heart, and for the hearts of all those who heard the sermon.

The sheep belong to the Good Shepherd, not to us. We have not bought them with our blood. And yet, we are called to serve them in love. Every preacher is a servant of the flock (pastors, of course, being undershepherds). We must go home thinking about the sheep and feeling for them. Our hearts must long that they hide the Word they've received in their hearts. We must realize, too, that the Devil works to snatch that Word away. Yes, we've discharged our responsibility in preaching. Is that it, though? Surely those filled with the Shepherd's love will feel compelled to pray that Christ would guard his Word by his Spirit in them and work silently for their great good in him. And so his will is done.

Post-sermon prayer is not our natural inclination. Before the sermon, things usually look different. We know we must preach as praying men. We seek to spend time praying during the week, and especially the morning before preaching, for everyone who will hear the sermon. And, of course, we pray in the pulpit to close our shared time in God's Word. Let's make sure that we are neither too relieved that the job's done nor too exhausted (or discouraged) to linger before the Lord when we get home, or later that day. Let's commit ourselves to praying in the lessons we've sought to teach our listeners. People need prayer.

We need prayer, too. Whether we've soared or crashed in our preaching, we are weak men, driven by thoughts and emotions that are all the stronger once the sermon's done. Temptations assault us, such as pride, despair, moroseness, and irritability. Of all people hearing the sermon, we ourselves are the most tempted to go home doubting it.

Try this preacher's prayer: *Lord, give me bread. Give me the bread of faith. Lord, I need your Spirit to fill me, to fight against my doubts, and to give me faith that the foolishness of preaching is your chosen means of doing your work. Lord, when my heart feels so empty of you and filled by the world, give me my daily bread. Fill me.*

Jesus is the Bread of Life (John 6:35). He alone can fill hearts. To pray for your daily bread is to pray for what your body needs each day. It's also to pray for what your soul needs, which is the grace of Christ. His presence can still racing thoughts, give hope for despairing preachers, and bring back restless, wandering desires to him. You believe that for your congregation, don't you? Believe it for yourself. And experience it as the gift of God to his praying children, including his preachers.

Such prayer means contentment.

42

Confession Time

Q. What's the worst sin we might commit in a sermon?
A. We preachers can be the greatest sinners by failing to proclaim God for who he is. So pray.

Forgive us our debts,
    as we also have forgiven our debtors.

Matthew 6:12

We preachers have all had good reason to be sorry for how we've preached. Yes, our lack of skill and gifting haunts us and has led to many a restless Sunday night, as we've been unable to shake off the memory of the day's failures. The failure runs deeper, though.

We've shown off our knowledge. We've wanted people to be impressed with our learning. In a day when the preacher struggles to get a hearing, knowledge is power, as we all know.

We've spoken out of anger and irritation. Even if it wasn't registered in our words or our tone. Even if no one's noticed it.

We've excused the unjustified anger of our hearts at a person or situation, and let it blaze a little more fiercely beneath the surface as we've preached.

We've made ourselves out to be better disciples than we are. We've remembered to tell our hearers again that we prayed for them the other day—for a long time. We've let slip how late at night it was that we set off to deal with some pastoral crisis, or how we returned from vacation for the sake of a needy person. We haven't told, though, about our own lapses of self-control, or the habitual complaining that defeats us. We've kept that covered up.

We've made others out to be worse disciples than they are. That "other church" has been subtly censored again. The struggling disciple we know (identity carefully disguised, of course) has become a convenient sermon illustration. We've failed to admire his perseverance under trial, though, and neglected to pray for him. His problems have served our purpose.

There are other sins, too, and many of them.

We've hurt, harmed, and maybe harangued people. We've bored them. We've confused and discouraged them. We preachers have committed enough pulpit sin to make us dread ever opening our Bibles in public again.

But our worst sin is that we've not proclaimed God as he is. That is the sin which burns behind all the others on our list. God has not been our first and our best thought and ambition as we've handled his Word. We've chased other goals, often not being aware of it. When God is absent, no amount of effort will make us declare his truth in Christ as we're called to.

Many a frustrated preacher, especially a pastor, turns up Revelation 3 with relish. The church you serve has disappointed you. They've not listened as you had hoped, and your preaching is not making the impact you had hoped and worked for. You conclude that it's all their fault, and you impatiently hunt for the remedy. Maybe you could take them to Laodicea?

Like the tepid, unhealthy spring water that ran into the city, believers there were dangerously lukewarm. They were so confident in themselves, they felt they didn't need the gospel. Christ himself sees a smugness that is trying to push him away and is close to disqualifying them from heaven. They need to open the door again to their Savior by a sincere repentance. So you look at your preaching and conclude that its frequent lack of penetration must be due to the Laodicean condition of your hearers. On occasion, you might be right. But what if it's the pulpit rather than the pew that needs to come back to the Lord? What if our sins actually show that we the preachers are the ones who are lukewarm?

Whether we're comfortable with it or not, we represent God to our hearers as we proclaim him. "Therefore, we are ambassadors for Christ, God making his appeal through us. We implore you on behalf of Christ, be reconciled to God" (2 Cor. 5:20). What sort of God do they hear and see as we preach?

We hope that they hear our words, the words we've thought carefully about in our preparation, and maybe have toiled over in polished paragraphs. And they *should* hear them as we expound God's Word. Listening, though, is far more than understanding another's words. Christians are listening to (and sometimes listening for) the preacher's heart. They hear what really drives him. They discover over time his weaknesses and his real loves. They see who he really is from his behavior, in the pulpit and out of it. Everyone knows that the preacher is one more struggling believer, an imperfect follower of the Master. Equally, they know that he is the Lord's ambassador. "Sir, we wish to see Jesus" (John 12:21) is the longing of believers. No Christian ever sees Jesus despite the preacher whose sins they must concentrate on ignoring; they see him in and through the preacher, or they do not see him at all.

This means that we have much work to do on our hearts. We have failed our hearers when we have failed to do battle with our personal sin and to put it to death. We have dishonored the King we serve if we come before his people in his name indifferent to the sins that cling to us.

Work starts on our knees, in prayer. Start with confession. "I have sinned" is a good place to begin dialogue with God. Confession is not merely good for the soul. Confession is, literally, life bringing. Confession doesn't save us from our sins—only Jesus does that—but without confession there can be no salvation. "Repent" isn't a command to wallow in guilt or play a misery game with God. It's a command to deal with guilt, or rather, to allow God to deal with guilt. Our guilt is real, actual, enslaving, joy robbing, and hell deserving. Deny it or justify it and it will kill us, slowly but surely. Come to Jesus and find it met, atoned for, washed away. The power is his, the coming is yours. That's your responsibility. Your repentance is the sure sign that you're believing the gospel in its grace.[1]

Beware of how your heart murmurs. Your sighs and complaints say everything about your real spiritual condition. Take some time today: write a list of the things you've heard yourself complaining about recently. Then write a list of reasons why you have no mandate to complain—ever. You are a child of God in Christ. He has won you at a great price. You belong to him—heart, mind, and body. Complaining hearts are cold hearts and need the fire of gospel grace again.

The preacher who repents will live and thrive. Try it. And the ministry that is bathed in repentance and enjoying renewing grace will be a truly gospel one, and will bear the hallmarks of authenticity.

The heart that knows this, knows that it belongs to Christ and lives in awe. We know that we can bring God nothing, we can earn no favor, and we can never out-sacrifice him, make him our debtor, or feel that anything we do merits his love. He is the Lord: holy, majestic, awesome. We come and we worship. Simply that. And then we rise off our knees to go and do his revealed will, in the power of the Spirit, to the praise of the Son—

> to do justice, and to love kindness,
>   and to walk humbly with [our] God. (Mic. 6:8)

---

1. Sinclair Ferguson helpfully observes that "faith will always be penitent; repentance will always be believing if genuine" (Ferguson, *The Whole Christ: Legalism, Antinomianism, and Gospel Assurance—Why the Marrow Controversy Still Matters* [Wheaton, IL: Crossway, 2016], 104n).

43

All for the King

Q. Will we pray ourselves into a glad submission to God?
A. Our preaching will never satisfy us. It isn't meant to. Let's give our hearts to God.

———

Yours, O LORD, is the greatness and the power and the glory and the victory and the majesty, for all that is in the heavens and in the earth is yours. Yours is the kingdom, O LORD, and you are exalted as head above all.

1 Chronicles 29:11

When we close the Lord's Prayer, we give honor to God, recognizing his kingdom, power, and glory. We do that, but the best Greek manuscripts that make up our Bibles don't actually contain the familiar ending of the prayer. There is no harm in praying that way, of course. That is essentially the same declaration as Psalm 103:19 and 1 Chronicles 29:11, that God really is the King enthroned in glory and might. He is the great reality for all of our praying, as well as our preaching. We must learn to declare to heaven that we submit our hearts to God's greatness in Jesus. We must learn to declare the same to our hearts. When our hearts bow joyfully to the King, then, and only then, will our preaching have any integrity and impact.

He's beautiful. Every page of Scripture tells us of a God who is holy and righteous. Ever page of gospel promise urges us to believe that this holy, righteous God gives himself entirely to us in the offer of the gospel. "I will be their God, and they shall be my people" (Ezek. 37:27) is the language of encounter, of love, and of experience, if it is anything. God loves us with a holy love. He wants us to know his love and to respond with the same to him.

Sometimes we preachers miss this. We lose hold of this love, the burning center of our commission to preach. And when we do, a tragedy starts to play out in our hearts. The tragedy is that we see God as a Master only. He is the Boss, while we are busily engaged (and often exhausted) in his work. We lose sight of the liberating truth that he is also lover, friend, encourager, comforter. This Master calls us to know him, and to share not just the work of the gospel but also the rest and the fellowship the gospel opens to us. What could be more tragic in the preacher's life but that he would wear himself away to skin and bone, starving himself of the very grace he seeks to proclaim to others?

Love only the work, and the work will crush us. Of course it will; the needs of a struggling church and a broken world are completely overwhelming. And while we effectively forget who God is in his gospel love, we will think that he achieves some satisfaction (some glory, even) in our being overworked and beaten down. But our fretful Saturdays, overwhelming Sundays, and washed-out Mondays might be less a symptom of zealous gospel faith and labor, and more a sign that we are anxiously slaving for God and man with little confidence and pleasure in God's sheer goodness.

We are wrong, dangerously wrong. He is not that sort of God. Ministry is not that sort of work. Preaching is the declaration of the God we know. Preaching is one broken sinner saying to others with exactly the same struggles, "This is the grace I'm discovering, which I long for you to know with me." And if the preacher and his preaching are captivated by this grace, then the life of the preacher will be one of humble, praise-filled joy.

What our people need most is our contentment. Listeners need to know that the preacher is contented in his God and rejoicing in his Savior. When our lives as preachers are filled with a sense of amazement about the grace that is ours in Christ, others start asking questions about that grace and seeking it for themselves. We may speak many words about God; but if our hearts are cold, how is the church to know if we believe our own words or not? The church needs to know that her teachers are men of praise and thanksgiving. Our own personal contentment in God's grace declares the power of the gospel to the church as well as the world, and shows the integrity of our hearts to God. God is looking for those who worship him in Spirit and in truth. Does he have such a worshiper in you?

Be careful of this word "contentment." It might sound to us like just a quiet little experience, self-contained and tucked in the corner, like a nervous Brit transplanted into a noisy American Fourth of July celebration. While contentment is often quiet, it also has a surprisingly loud voice, and it's the voice of praise. You can see and you can hear when people are contented. The church can see and hear when those in the pulpit are delighting in Christ and satisfied in him. True contentment is as powerful as it is visible.

One day we will open our mouths to God in the presence of his glory. Will we argue, complain, rage, or question? Of course not. We will confess that he is the Lord, and we will bow down in worship. Our eyes will see him. We will be satisfied, and delighted, as we lay ourselves before him and hear his voice.

Heaven is the home of all our lasting happiness.

And so we dare to pursue contentment in God. We dare believe that there is such a place of settled joy and peace in Jesus. We really can make him our treasure when life and ministry are painful, as much as when they are exciting. We can, and we must. To him be the glory, forever.

Scripture Index